A SH

OF CLASSIC

ALIS

Alasdair Gray was born in Glasgow in 1934. He was educated at Whitehill Senior Secondary School and studied drawing and painting at the Glasgow School of Art from 1952–7. After Art School he worked as a part-time art teacher and on commissions for portraits and murals. During this time he was also writing short stories and a semi-autobiographical novel which changed and developed through several drafts over the course of twenty years, to become *Lanark*. After training at Jordanhill in 1960 he taught art in Glasgow schools for the next two years before going on to make a difficult living as an artist, a writer, a scene painter and part-time lecturer. Gray married Inge Sørensen in 1962 and the couple had a son in 1964 but were divorced in 1970. In 1968 his play *The Fall of Kelvin Walker* was broadcast on BBC TV. In the 1970s Gray was attending Glasgow University lecturer Philip Hobsbaum's creative writing sessions, in a group which included Tom Leonard, Liz Lochhead and James Kelman. During this period he wrote several plays for radio and television, some of which were done on stage, while he continued to paint and to work on murals. (Some of his murals can still be seen at Palace Rigg Nature Reserve in Cumbernauld, in Abbots House local history museum in Dunfermline, and in the

Ubiquitous Chip restaurant in Glasgow.) Gray's first novel, *Lanark*, was published by Canongate in 1981 to widespread critical acclaim, followed by short stories in *Unlikely Stories, Mostly* (1983), a second major novel *1982 Janine* (1984), *The Fall of Kelvin Walker* as a novel (1985), and *Lean Tales* (with Agnes Owens and James Kelman) in the same year.

Gray's work is characterised by an exuberant imaginative energy, which uses fantasy and fabulation to good-humoured effect, while never losing sight of his darker and more critical sense of the effects of personal, cultural, and political alienation in the modern world. Technically his books make free use of meta-narrative games, typographical effects, mock scholarly addenda and his own fine and complex illustrations.

Gray produced a brief *Saltire Self Portrait* in 1988 and a collection of poems, *Old Negatives*, appeared in 1989, with *McGrotty and Ludmilla* (the novel version of a play written in 1975) and the novel *Something Leather* in 1990. A wholly original revision of the Frankenstein theme featured in the novel *Poor Things* (1992) and further short stories were published as *Ten Tales True and Tall* (1993), with two further books *A History Maker* (1994) and *Mavis Belfrage* (1996). A polemical essay *Why Scots Should Rule Scotland* was published in 1992 and revised in 1997. His most recent work is *An Anthology of Prefaces* (2000). Gray's fiction has been translated into more than a dozen languages throughout the world, including Lithuanian, Polish, Czech, Japanese, Swedish and Serbo-Croatian.

A SHORT SURVEY OF CLASSIC SCOTTISH WRITING

Alasdair Gray

7

CANONGATE POCKET CLASSICS

First published as a Pocket Classic in 2001 by Canongate Books Ltd, 14 High Street, Edinburgh EH1 1TE.

10 9 8 7 6 5 4 3 2 1

The publishers gratefully acknowledge subsidy from the Scottish Arts Council towards the Canongate Classics and Pocket Classics series.

Typeset in 10 pt Plantin by Palimpsest Book Production Limited, Polmont, Stirlingshire.

Printed and bound by Omnia Books, Glasgow.

British Library Cataloguing-in-Publication Data
A catalogue record for this volume is available on request from the British Library

ISBN 1 84195 167 6

www.canongate.net

Contents

TO TOM LEONARD

On God the Tree's Scottish branch new buds grow.
The blighted prove it is no dead stick.
You flower and fruit,
drop seeds that take root.

Foreword

FOLK WHO READ for pleasure have this in common with scholars: they will not confine their reading to the books of one nation if they understand the speech of more. In his collection of 18th-century Scots lyrics Thomas Crawford says that out of three thousand or so books printed in Scotland from 1682 to 1785 some two thousand were in English speech, including many by Englishmen; and in cheaper publications for mass consumption half the tales and songs were on English or Irish topics. Scots-English traffic passed in both directions. Queen Anne annoyed Henry Purcell, her court musician, by preferring *Cold and Raw*, a popular Scottish song, to one of his. The first Kilmarnock edition of Burns's poems was printed the following year in London, Dublin, New York and Philadelphia. Wordsworth, Keats and Byron acknowledged his genius and influence; Matthew Arnold thought him second only to Chaucer.

No imagination can limit itself to a single national

idea without growing stupider, like Nazis who rejected the work of Heine and Mendelssohn because they were Jewish, so why should readers who can enjoy the dialects of Shakespeare, Burns and Mark Twain fix their attention, for the duration of this short book, upon writing made within a single national boundary? — Because after Arnold the teaching of literature in British universities allocated most Scottish writing to a footnote or ignored it. Walter Scott was accepted as an honorary Englishman because his influence throughout Europe could not be ignored, but Hogg and Galt were mainly ignored. For most of his creative life so was Hugh MacDiarmid. *The Oxford Book of Sixteenth Century Verse* edited by Emrys Jones in 1991 should have *In England* added to the title because it leaves out William Dunbar, Gavin Douglas, David Lindsay, Drummond of Hawthornden – every Scots poet of that period. Specialists in south British writing would have done no harm in the south, but Scottish education employed too many of them in the north. A Glasgow University lecturer of the 1970s used to call Burns *a poor man's Alexander Pope.* This attitude became so notorious in the teaching of literature AND history that in the latter part of the 20th century Scottish universities had to cure it by creating special departments of Scottish Studies. They could not enlarge existing history and literature courses to include Scottish life and letters because these were mostly run by English nationalists who did not know their own limitations, and used text books that reinforced them. The roots of Scottish literature had mainly survived through the interest of French, German and American scholars, also a few native enthusiasts: MacDiarmid, Agnes Mure Mackenzie, William Power and John Speirs who wrote surveys like this one to enlarge, not limit, the number of books their readers might enjoy.

These surveys often presented Scots literature as a growth stunted by catastrophe, a grim view got by comparing Scotland's literary history, not with that of Germany, Poland or other nations that had suffered equal or worse turmoils, but by comparing it with England after 1700. This was not an England torn by Norman barons, peasant revolt, Plantagenet or Parliamentary civil war; but England when a stable ruling class was enlarging or profiting by a worldwide commercial empire. Most of this class and its prospering subjects took their nation for granted – saw nothing questionable in it. Even during the 1914–18 war when millions of British were being slaughtered overseas, public posters in London proudly announced BUSINESS AS USUAL. No other combatant nation could take such losses so calmly. That war made most of the other nations reinvent themselves, starting with Ireland. France had been reinventing herself since the revolution of 1790.

Many Scots, of course, were junior partners in England's imperial business venture. It enriched them, but they felt uneasy about Scotland's subordinate position and feared their culture was dying. They cultivated nostalgia while their historians blamed the demise on events now beyond human control: the Protestant Reformation, Union of Crowns, Union of Parliaments, the Industrial Revolution or Modernisation. This elegiac patriotism was ended by the good work of folk I name later in this book, which tries to tell how poets and narrators peacefully reinvented Scots culture from early times to the 20th century. My account often speaks of England's state, for the two states are bound to act on each other, though the northern state is most aware of this.

Like all short books on big intricate matters this is a hopscotch survey, leaping from one classic work to another across many that deserve study too. By classic I mean what D.H. Lawrence implies in his *Study of Classic American Literature*: the best. What I think best is limited, of course, by my taste and education, and having spoken of other writers' limitations I will declare my own.

This book's most glaring defect comes from my ignorance of Gaelic, the original speech of the Scottish nation and until the 13th century the dominant one. Poets have kept it alive as a literary language from at least 600 AD to the present day, despite the antagonism of governments who have made it the speech of a minority. Several Gaelic poets were and are women, more women than are found in many other literatures before the 20th century. This makes my failure here more deplorable. I do not wholly ignore Gaelic writing, but all my references to it are both second-hand and inadequate.

I should have said much more about Hume, Smith, Hutton and other 18th-century writers, giving and discussing examples of their work. The same is true of later novelists. If I one day enlarge this book, preferably working with a Gaelic scholar-poet, I will mend these omissions and many others.

I had meant the last chapter to deal with folk who are still alive and writing in March 2001, but none whose first books were published after 1980. That cut-off rule would have let me avoid mentioning *Lanark* (a grossly over-rated novel) and stopped me picking and choosing among a multitude of fascinating contemporaries while letting me discuss writers who have been my friends for a quarter century. There was no time for me to do that, so the last writers discussed in detail did their best work before my birth in 1934. This may save the book from some adverse criticism. Sir Walter Raleigh's *History of the World* stops far short of his own time because, he says in his preface, *Who-so-ever writes a moderne Historie that shall follow truth too near the heeles, it may happily strike out his teeth.* By *happily* he meant possibly – not cheerfully.

A final warning to anyone with a good memory who knows my other non-fiction works. You will find passages here that you have read before. My mind has not improved with age so I cannot describe the same things again in better words.

Alasdair Gray
March 2001

CHAPTER ONE

Land, Language and Early Literature

NATIONS ARE MADE by folk in a particular kind of land reacting to each other and to neighbours outside, so any good atlas will show why a country's way of life, government and writing differ from those of neighbouring lands, if it shows differences of soil and climate.

The Scottish end of the British archipelago has a grotesquely irregular mainland with a multitude of peninsulas and islands to the west. The tip of the most southerly peninsula is only twelve miles from the Irish coast; the nearest neighbour on the European mainland is Norway, with the Orkney and Shetland islands like stepping-stones between. Inside Scotland's ragged coastline the glens and plains are so separated by highland sea-lochs and mountains, lowland moors and firths, that cultivation could never produce great wealth for a great many, and the natural barriers made conquest of the whole place impossible for invaders. But south of a forty-mile line joining the Solway and Tweed is a larger country where bigger plains, thicker soil and milder climate allowed the cultivation of wealth worth plundering, while fewer natural barriers made it harder to defend. A narrow sea divides the south east coast from a busy part of Europe, so by 400 AD those mighty plunderers, the Romans, had covered south Britain with a network of military roads joining all but Wales to the southern seaports and the great market of London. When Rome pulled out its legions the ex-colony was chopped into several nations by German and Danish invaders who spoke varieties of Anglo-Saxon.

North Britain at that time had fewer kingdoms but more languages. A Welsh dialect was spoken in Galloway and the midland belt. The coastal plain and dales between Forth and Tweed were occupied by Anglo-Saxons from Northumbria. North of the Forth and Clyde lived people the Romans had called Picts. Caithness, Sutherland, Orkney and many western isles were seized by Norwegian earls, while Irish settlers had founded a Gaelic kingdom in Argyll. These Gaels were the first Scots on the British mainland, also the first Christian nation there, because Ireland, the part of Britain Rome never invaded, was the part where Christianity and literature most flourished after Rome left. Monks from Ireland and St Columba's abbey on Iona were christianising Pictland and Northumbria in 597 when a mission sent by Pope Gregory landed in Kent and its leader, Saint Augustine, became first Archbishop of Canterbury. The seven English kingdoms thus gained a hierarchy of parish priests appointed by bishops, who were themselves approved by Canterbury, and were set on a way toward greater prosperity and unity. That was possible in the south because the old Roman roads, though badly maintained, were still useful trade routes linking at least twelve towns that began slow, erratic growth into big modern cities.

North Britain then had no such towns. The seats of her kings were huddles of low buildings on the ancient volcanic plugs of Dunadd, Dumbarton and Edinburgh, so northern Christianity was spread by monks who lived on lands they farmed. Partly by military skill, partly by intermarriage, but mainly through support by the Celtic church, the Scots gave their name to most of Britain north of Solway and Tweed in 1054, but for long afterwards the Scottish settlements most resembling towns were monasteries surrounded by their farmlands, with a church, sleeping quarters, school, mill, workshops and warehouses. Monks in Scotland were the first to mine coal, distil whisky and write books. Their industry made the growth of adjacent towns possible.

But before 1066 the Scotland-England difference in urban wealth indicated no huge difference in political structures and artistic skill. All British kings were warlords heading alliances of clans or settlements. Though nearly all illiterate (only King Alfred of Wessex wrote books) they had a civil service of clergy using the phonetic Roman alphabet which still records and preserves the vernacular literature of western Europe and America. Local chiefs also employed fine woodworkers, metalworkers and stonecarvers, even in Pictland, which is sometimes dismissed as a cultural desert because no good record of its language survives. But all kings and great chieftains employed poets to praise their ancestors, and their achievements, and lament their defeats.

These bards, skalds or skops (as they were variously called) used many complex verse forms, for they had to learn and chant the best works of earlier poets before adding to them. Southern bards usually followed Roman Virgil's example and traced the ancestors of their tribes back to the Trojan war. Gaelic bards followed the bible's example and traced them through Ireland, Spain, Africa and Palestine to the Garden of Eden. In a long poem called *The Gododdin* the Welsh bard

Aneurin describes the battle by which an Anglo-Saxon alliance defeated the northern Welsh whose capital was Edinburgh. The greatest flowering of literature happened in Northumbria, where the Gaelic and English clergy came together and (after some argument, for Gaels had founded the first monasteries there) blended. In Lindisfarne, Jarrow and Whitby the clergy made gospel-books in a style sometimes called Hiberno-Saxon, meaning Irish-English. Initial letters were surrounded and filled with Celtic scrolls and spirals inlaid with gold and jewelled colours, but the language of their vernacular literature was Anglo-Saxon. Northumbrian priests wrote the first English poems describing how God made heaven, hell and earth, and glorifying Christ on the cross. This last poem (*The Dream of the Rood*) has also been claimed for Scotland, as parts are carved on a splendid monument at Ruthwell, north of the Solway. Meanwhile Scottish and Northumbrian clergy wrote hymns and history in Latin, and Norwegian skalds wrote sagas describing the violent politics of Orkney. Norse bishops and saints in those days carried swords and shed blood, so they despised as womanish the Gaelic and Saxon clergy who did not.

But vernacular poets throughout Britain spoke

the same language, were of the same people as the kings and chiefs employing them. The Norman conquest changed that.

Note

Canongate Classic no. 86, *The Triumph Tree*, edited by Thomas Owen Clancy, 1998, prints translations of Scotland's earliest poetry in Latin, Welsh, Gaelic, Old English and Norse, from AD 550 to 1350.

CHAPTER TWO

Freedom and Barbour's Bruce

A NATION HAS been defined as a dialect with an army to defend it, which was certainly true of England after 1066. The self-perpetuating class of Norman-French officers who now owned it conferred and wrote laws in a French dialect, for they still owned parts of France and fought for centuries to conquer the rest. No great national literature is possible where rulers speak a different language from the ruled, or where speech cannot be freely shared. The Anglo-Saxon subjects of Norman barons forgot their earliest literature while their speech and their landlords' speech was merging into a new one. Over two centuries passed before the rulers of England agreed to be English. By then they had a thriving middle class with a say in parliamentary government, and inns where prosperous tradesmen and merchants mixed with knights and abbots, as Chaucer describes in his *Canterbury Tales*. Most literary forms used in England AND south Scotland were introduced by Chaucer, a civil servant who entered literature by translating love poems, allegories and novellas out of French and Italian.

The freedom of speech which made Chaucer's poetry possible was based upon a new level of prosperity, a prosperity chiefly derived from England's wool exports, a prosperity even English peasants thought they could share before the government crushed their march on London. Before the 17th century Scotland had no surplus of anything to export apart from folk who wanted a better life outside it. Those who stayed at home had to base their kind of freedom on shared hardship.

War is a great uniter of social classes, and between 1073 and 1560 Scotland and England were usually at war. The northern population was then (as now) less than an eighth of the southern, but neither side could win. England's richest land and most productive people were in the south, which the small Scottish armies never reached. Scots people and wealth were also mainly in the south, so large English armies invaded there again and again, but could not defeat folk who burned their own crops, retreated into wildernesses and lived rough until the invaders left. Trade was ruined, towns stopped growing but free speech flourished. A French visitor (Froissart) thought it remarkable that if a knight rode his horse over a Scots grainfield an angry peasant ran up and cursed him. No peasants dared to do that in rich lands where the nobility had hundreds of workers so could have one flogged or hung without loss of income. Scots lairds were so poor they needed ALL their peasants and grain crops. Greater freedom at a tougher level of existence was the result, and a middle class that still mainly consisted of clergy who were passionately patriotic, having no wish to be ruled from Canterbury. In 1296 Scotland's king and nobility agreed to let Edward of England rule them. Edward sent in English troops and governors to make sure he did, so most of the Scots people and clergy drove these out by supporting the guerilla fighters, Wallace and Bruce. Bruce's final victories at last united the Scots nobility behind him. Two Scottish priests wrote great works about that achievement.

The first is a masterpiece of political persuasion written in 1320 by Bernard de Linton, Abbot of Arbroath and Chancellor of Scotland, and sent to a pope who did not think Bruce fit to rule. Though signed by many nobles it claimed to be written *on behalf of the whole community of the realm of Scotland.* It said Bruce was now king of the Scots because he was helping them win free of English oppression, but if he stopped doing so *we shall exert ourselves to drive him out as our enemy, and an underminer of his own rights and ours, and will make another man who is able to defend us our king . . . For as long as a hundred of us stay alive, we will never submit to being brought under English rule. It is in truth not for glory, or for riches, or for honours we are fighting, but for freedom, which no good man loses except with his life.* This was written in fluent Latin, the language of international diplomacy, four and a half centuries before the

ORIGINAL VERSION

Storys to rede ar delitabill
suppos that that be nocht bot fabill
than suld storys that suthfast wer
and thai war said on gud maner
have doubill plesance in heryng
the first plesance is the carpyng
and the tother the suthfastness
that schawys the thing rycht as it wes

American Declaration of Independence, at a time when kings thought their nations were inherited properties, and most landlords and clergy supported that idea. Yet the Pope was persuaded.

The second masterpiece is *The Bruce*, 13,500 lines of rhyming couplets, eight syllables per line, written around 1370 (and about ten years before *The Canterbury Tales*) by John Barbour, a diplomat who became Archdeacon of Aberdeen. It cannot be the oldest poem in Lowland Scots but is the oldest to survive, and a rarity in any language. It combines factual history and heroic fiction in equal measure, starting thus:

MODERN TRANSLATION

Stories to read are delightable,
supposing they be nought but fable;
then should stories that truthful were,
be they said in good manner,
give double pleasure in the hearing.
the first pleasure is the telling,
the other in the truthfulness
Which shows the thing right as it was:

and suth thyngis that are likand
tyll mannys heryng ar plesand,
tharfor I wald fayne set my will
giff my wyt mycht suffice thartill
to put in wryt a suthfast story
that it lest ay furth in memory
swa that na tyme of lenth it let
na ger it haly be forget
for auld storys that men redys
representis to thaim the dedys
of stalwart folk that lywyt ar
rycht as thai than in presence war
and certis thai suld weill have prys
that in thar tyme war wycht and wys
and led thar lyff in gret trawaill
and oft in hard stour off bataill
wan gret price off chewalry
and war woydyt off cowardy
as wes king robert off Scotland,
that hardy wes off hart and hand

Then we hear how Scotland suffered under English misrule and how Bruce, who had sworn loyalty to England's king, cheats him and gets crowned king of Scots after murdering Comyn, his rival for the job. Bruce has therefore to fight his victim's relations and allies as well as the English, so wins

and true things that are likened
to suit man's hearing are pleasant,
therefore I would set my will
(if that my wit suffice theretill)
to put in writ a truthful story,
so that it lasts in memory,
and that no length of time it rot,
or lets it wholly be forgot,
for old stories that men reads
represent to them the deeds
of stalwart folk that lively were
just as if they in presence are;
and certain it is we should prize
who in their time were weighty, wise,
and led their life in great trouble
and oft in hard dirt of battle
won right great prize from chivalry
and voided were of cowardy
as was King Robert of Scotland
that hardy was of heart and hand

nothing by his first battles and loses control of the country. He retreats to the wilderness round Loch Lomond; parts company with his noble allies, his wife, his horse; becomes a hunted outlaw on foot, fleeing with a handful of followers. He survives and his followers increase. They raid castles throughout

Scotland: castles which are now ruins but were then centres of power. Any Scottish army Bruce musters is always outnumbered by England's, so he only fights battles on ground he has chosen and knows better than the invaders. He is finally victorious. The historic truth of this outline is confirmed by contemporary documents, most of them English.

But this poem was commissioned by King Robert II who wanted his predecessor glorified as a national hero. In Jewish, Greek, Roman and Hindu writings such heroes are warriors guided by Jehovah or other Gods who prophesy and aid their success. Later heroes like Beowulf, King Arthur, French Roland, German Parsifal etc. are involved with monsters and miracles. Only heroes of Norse sagas occupy plausible worlds without spooky interference. Scotland's close dealings with Norway in Barbour's day perhaps introduced him to the sagas; but he also worked when many who had known Bruce still lived. Small nations are sceptical about their rulers, even victorious ones. Barbour's poem managed to praise Bruce in ways that allow scepticism about the beauty of his character. It says Bruce killed Comyn because the latter had betrayed his plans to Edward, but adds that some folk believe a different story. He describes Bruce and Earl

Douglas, his greatest supporter, as both gentle and chivalrous, yet shows that the first is moved by unscrupulous ambition, and that the second would have submitted to Edward if Edward had not seized his lands. As the war continues he shows the rules of chivalry abandoned by both sides, who start butchering defeated foes of every rank. Barbour, a priest, has Bruce declare that God will support the Scots because they fight to keep their own land while the English fight to steal it. He never suggests Bruce has supernatural aid.

Barbour's verse lacks the metrical variety of Langland, Chaucer and the Gawaine poet, his English contemporaries, nor does it evoke the richly bustling societies they describe, but it tells an exciting story with something better than the speed and directness of good prose, and heightens the excitement where needed: in the clash and bloodshed of battle, the beauty of a fine May morning, the movement of rowing boats over a surging sea. A long poem must succeed by more than a few fine passages and a long work, however full of incidents, is second-rate without a grand or satirical idea uniting them. Barbour's unifying idea is given near the start.

BARBOUR'S VERSE

A! Fredome is a noble thing,
Fredome mays man to haiff liking.
Fredome all solace to man giffis,
He levys at es that frely levys.
A noble hart may haiff nane es
Na ellys nocht that may him ples
Gyff fredome failyhe . . .

Barbour later likens Bruce to Scipio, a general who, when Hannibal was marching upon Rome and the richest citizens wanted to flee, saved the city by freeing slaves and making knights of these and the servant class so they stood ready to support him. This anticipates the battle of Bannockburn where Bruce lets his outnumbered soldiers choose to fight or not. They choose to fight, and the tide of battle turns for them when the Scots camp servants, waving poles and sheets, join the fight and the English mistake them for a huge enemy reinforcement.

The poem's defects as a work of art are too many episodes where Bruce with a single helper and outnumbered by three or four enemies, predictably kills them without suffering a scratch. Its main

MODERN TRANSLATION

A! Freedom is a noble thing,
Freedom lets man have his liking.
Freedom all solace to man gives,
He lives at ease who freely lives.
A noble heart may have no ease
Nor anything that may him please
If freedom fail . . .

defect as history is its refusal to mention William Wallace, who led a rising of commoners that almost drove the invaders out of Scotland when Bruce was still King Edward's obedient servant. Wallace showed Bruce that victory was possible. Wallace always embarrasses writers who think only noblemen deserve to be heroes.

Note

Canongate Classic no. 78, *The Bruce* by John Barbour, edited with introduction, prose translation and notes by Archie A. M. Duncan, 1997. This contains a full translation of the Declaration of Arbroath.

CHAPTER THREE

Six More Makers

IF WE IGNORE Gaelic, *The Bruce* is almost the one work of Scots poetry made during the age of great imaginative writing sometimes called Middle English, for it comes between the Anglo-Saxon and the modern period begun by Elizabethan drama, sometimes called the Chaucerian age since Chaucer lived through it. After Chaucer's death in

THE KING'S WORDS

Quhare, in a lusty plane, tuke I my way,
  Endlang a ryver, plesant to behold,
Enbroudin all with fresche flouris gay,
  Quhare, throu the gravel, bryght as any gold,
  The cristall water ran so clere and cold,
That in myn ere maid contynualy
A maner soun, mellit with armony;

That full of lytill fischis by the brym,

1400, south British writing (if we ignore Wales) lacked originality for well over a century. The cause is outside the scope of this book. But Victorian scholars noticed fine work by several north British poets writing from about 1470 to 1520 and, because they praised Chaucer and had learned much from him, called them the Scottish Chaucerians: which was like calling Thackeray, the Brontës and George Eliot the English Scottians, because they praised and learned much from Walter Scott.

But before describing and quoting from Henryson, Dunbar and the rest I give this verse of a poem written between Chaucer's time and theirs, for comparison.

MODERN TRANSLATION

Where, on a lusty plain, took I my way
  Along a river, pleasant to behold,
Embroidered all with freshest flowers gay,
  Where, through the gravel, bright as any gold,
  The crystal water ran so clear and cold,
That in my ear it made continually
A gentle sound, sweetened with harmony;

And full of little fishes by the brim,

Now here, now there, with bakkis blewe as
lede,
Lap and playit, and in a rout can swym
So prattily, and dressit tham to sprede
Thair curall fynnis, as the ruby rede,
That in the sonne on their scalis bryght
As gesserant ay glitterit in my sight.

The above is from *The King's Quair* – The King's Book – a poem by James I in the allegory of love mode that British and French courtiers greatly enjoyed for its combination of religious and amorous delight. The setting is a beautiful landscape, usually walled or hedged round, where lovers meet in perfect safety and harmony, at once The Garden of Eden and a palace boudoir. It often appeared in prayerbook illustrations and tapestries too, and the

HENRYSON'S WORDS

That samin seasoun, in to ane soft morning,
Rycht blyth that bitter blastis were ago,
Unto the wod, to see the flouris spring,
And heir the Mavis sing and birdis mo,
I passit ffurth syne lukit to and ffro,
To se the Soill that was richt sessonabill,
Sappie, and to resave all seidis abill.

> Now here, now there, with backs as blue as
> lead,
> They leapt and played, and in a riot swim
> So prettily, and dressed themselves to spread
> Their coral fins, like to the ruby red,
> That in the sun, upon their scales so bright,
> It glittered like scale-armour in my sight.

riverbank embroidered with *fresche flouris gay* suggests tapestry. The running, sounding water and playful, glittering fish keep the scene lively while the use of gold, crystal, ruby, etc. give it a dreamlike richness, as the poet intended.

Compare these verses by Robert Henryson, a priest and schoolmaster employed at Dunfermline Abbey:

MODERN TRANSLATION

> In that same season, on a soft morning,
> Right blyth that bitter blasts were now ago,
> Unto the wood, to see the flowers spring,
> And hear the thrush and other birds also,
> I wandered forth and then looked to and fro
> To see the Soil that was right seasonable,
> Sappy, and to receive all seeds right able.

Moving thusgait, grit myrth I tuke in mynd,
Offlauboraris to se the besines,
Sum makand dyke, and sum the pleuch can
wynd,
Sum sawand seidis fast ffrome place to place,
The Harrowis hoppand in the saweris trace:
It was grit Joy to him that luifit corne,
To se thame laubour, baith at even and morne.

This reminds me of Turgenev's saying that only farmers and hunters truly appreciate a landscape, meaning, only those who skilfully cultivate and use a land to feed themselves and others can truly know and perhaps love what it is. Poets who describe it without that degree of knowledge are seeing it as a mere pleasure park in good weather, a mere annoyance or test of character at other times. Henryson served an abbey where corn was grown, reaped, ground, baked and eaten. His use of a capital S in *Soil* is as deliberate as the capital G in God. His grasp of earthy necessities underlay his good humour, sympathy, and social insight.

These show best in his fourteen *Moral Fables* where selfishly strong and cunning folk in church and state are satirised as wolf and fox, legal practitioners as raven, hawk and vulture, the stupidly

Moving this way, great mirth I took in mind
Of labourers seeing the busyness,
Some digging ditches, some the plough to
wind,
Some sowing seeds swiftly from place to place,
The harrows hopping in the sowers trace:
It was great joy to him that loves the corn
To see them labour, both at even and morn.

proud and lecherous as cocks and hens. This provides excellent slapstick comedy when rogues defeat bullies or both undermine themselves, but Henryson has a tender regard for mice, small birds and animals who represent the vulnerable part of humanity. A dog falsely accuses a sheep of owing him money for bread. After a lengthy court case the sheep is found guilty, cannot afford to appeal, and must sell its fleece to pay the dog, the legal birds of prey and the wolf who judges the case. The naked victim, shivering in a snowdrift, is left praying *Lord God why sleepest thou so long?* This end is not funny nor meant to be. Henryson knew how the law and foul weather strike defenceless souls and says the sheep represents the *pure commounis* – poor commoners – in a land where love, loyalty and justice can be bought and sold.

His human decency is equally shown in *The Testament of Cresseid*, the sequel he wrote to Chaucer's *Troilus and Cressida*, which has been called the first psychological novel. Chaucer's tale ends with the heroine estranged from her first true lover and living as his enemy's mistress. Henryson presents himself as old, no longer capable of love, brooding on what became of Cresseid later. His sequel has her thrown out by her second man and returning to her father who treats her kindly. She curses Cupid and Venus for bringing her to such grief, and in return for that blasphemy the gods give her leprosy. Though full of rich detail the poem does not gloat over the punishment of a faithless woman: the poetry is in the pity for some-one (Henryson suggests) whose fate is like his own: early experience and hopes of love lost through change (old age in his case) arriving as a disease.

James IV had both a Gaelic and a lowland Scots laureate. Dunbar was the latter, and this is his most popular poem: I have removed five verses. The Latin line means *fear of death dismays me*; *brukle* = breakable, *sle* = sly, *sicker* = certain, *wicker* = willow, *stour* = the cloud of dirt kicked up by conflict, *piscence* = wealth, *lechis* = leeches, doctors who remove blood. More translation is surely needless.

DUNBAR'S LAMENT FOR THE MAKERS
(when he was sick)

I that in heill wes and gladnes,
Am trublit now with gret seiknes,
And feblit with infermite;
Timor mortis conturbat me.

Our plesance heir is all vane glory,
This fals warld is bot transitory,
The flesche is brukle, the Fend is sle;
Timor mortis conturbat me.

The stait of man dois change and vary,
Now sound, now seik, now blith, now sary,
Now dansand mery, now like to dee;
Timor mortis conturbat me.

No stait in erd heir standis sicker;
As with the wynd wavis the wicker,
Wavis the warldis vanite;
Timor mortis conturbat me.

On to the ded gois all Estatis,
Princis, Prelotis, and Potestatis,
Baith riche and pur of al degre;
Timor mortis conturbat me.

He takis the knychtis in to field,
Anarmit under helm and scheild;
Victour he is at all mellie;
Timor mortis conturbat me.

That strang unmercifull tyrand
Takis, on the moderis breist sowkand,
The bab full of benignite;
Timor mortis conturbat me.

He takis the campion in the stour,
The capitaine closit in the tour,
The lady in bour full of bewte;
Timor mortis conturbat me.

He sparis no lord for his piscence,
Na clerk for his intelligence;
His awfull strak may no man fle;
Timor mortis conturbat me.

Art-magicianis, and astrologgis,
Rethoris, logicianis, and theologgis,
Thame helpis no conclusionis sle;
Timor mortis conturbat me.

In medicyne the most practicianis,
Lechis, surrigianis, and physicianis,
Thame self fra ded may not supple;
Timor mortis conturbat me.

I se that makaris amang the laif
Playis heir their pageant, syne gois to graif;
Sparit is nocht ther faculte;
Timor mortis conturbat me.

He hes done petuously devour,
The noble Chaucer, of makaris flour,
The monk of Bery, and Gower, all thre;
Timor mortis conturbat me.

That scorpion fell hes done infeck
Maister Johne Clerk, and James Affleck,
Fra balat making and tragedie;
Timor mortis conturbat me.

Holland and Barbour he hes berevit:
Allace! that he nocht with us levit
Schir Mungo Lokert of the Le:
Timor mortis conturbat me.

He hes Blind Hary and Sandy Traill
Slaine with his schour of mortall haill,
Quhilk Patrik Johnstoun myght nocht fle:
  Timor mortis conturbat me.

In Dunfermelyne he hes done roune
With Maister Robert Henrisoun;
Schir Johne the Ros enbrast hes he;
  Timor mortis conturbat me.

Gud Maister Walter Kennedy
In poynt of dede lyis veraly,
Gret reuth it wer that so suld be;
  Timor mortis conturbat me.

Sen he hes all my brether tane,
He will nocht lat me lif alane,
On forse I Man his nyst pray be;
  Timor mortis conturbat me.

Sen for the deid remeid is none,
Best is that we for dede dispone,
Eftir our deid that lif may we;
  Timor mortis conturbat me.

James IV allowed a freedom of speech that was fatal to all who used it near his English brother-in-law, Henry VIII. Dunbar's verse denounces greedy lawyers, clergy, courtiers and the king's favourites; laments his own empty purse, his headaches, the filthy streets of Edinburgh and the damnably changeable Scots weather; he also wrote hymns, allegories and a poem on James's marriage in the ornate style of *The King's Quair*. His longest poem, *The Treatis of the Twa Mariit Women and the Wedo*, starts on a warm mid-summer evening beside a flowering garden hedged with hawthorns where a bird sings *sugariit* melody and three blossom-crowned, golden-haired, laughing ladies talk about love. The Eden-like harmony shatters when we hear their words, for it is marital love and disgusts all three. One says her young husband has so used up his virility on whores that his prick can hardly stand after seven weeks' rest, yet he struts about as if still God's gift to all women, like a dog lifting his leg at every tree though there is no piss left in him. That is only one of the complaints. Victorian critics thought this discussion offensive to female decency. Modern feminists may think it an accurate account of male weaknesses.

To handle his variety of subjects in sweet, comic, satirical or sober tones Dunbar used many verse forms, rhyme patterns and metres. To support these he enlarged his Scots vocabulary with words coined out of Latin and French. That is why Hugh MacDiarmid advised modern Scottish poets to learn their craft by studying Dunbar.

But the greatest single work made in Renaissance Scotland was completed in 1513 by the Reverend Father Gavin Douglas, Bishop of Dunkeld, who wrote the first British translation of Virgil's *Aeneid.* Written twenty years before Jesus was born, the *Aeneid* described the legendary founding of Rome and foretold that her empire would establish universal peace. Christianity had been spread through that empire, Rome had become the capital of Christendom, so Virgil's poem, like the bible, seemed to foretell Christ's second coming. For over a millennium in Europe literate folk believed that only the bible was a greater book than the *Aeneid.* A good translator needed to be an excellent Latin scholar besides an excellent poet, as confident in the speech of his own nation as Virgil had been in his. Dante and Chaucer were such poets, but having chiefly learned their craft by translating French poetry into their own tongues had preferred inventing new long poems of their own, though Dante used Virgil as his guide and example.

Douglas retold each event of the *Aeneid* in the order Virgil gave with the same similes and metaphors, despite which his translation is also a new long poem of his own. Virgil's Latin was the clear, highly refined speech of an aristocracy who efficiently managed an empire containing every nation surrounding the Mediterranean. The language of Douglas was spoken by about half the people in a Scotland containing hardly more than 500,000. He belonged to one of the ten or twelve ruling families there because his dad was an earl, but his nation was so poor that its kings sometimes murdered enemies with their own hands since they could not (like French and English kings) trust agents to do it. In his Prologue to the translation Douglas attacks previous translations, especially a prose version by Caxton, also Chaucer's verse account of the Dido episode, though he praises Chaucer for being the most glorious of all modern poets. Then Douglas praises Virgil's perfectly polished, exact speech, says that love moves him to write something tasting of the *Aeneid* in his own *rural vulgar gross* language, then tells the reader –

FROM THE AENEID PROLOGUE

Fyrst I protest, beaw schirris, be your leif,
Beis weill avisit my wark or yhe repreif,
Consider it warly, reid oftar than anys;
Weill at a blenk sle poetry nocht tayn is,
And yit forsuyth I set my bissy pane
As that I couth to mak it braid and plane,
Kepand na sudron bot our awyn langage,
And spekis as I lernyt quhen I was page.
Nor yit sa cleyn all sudron I refuss,
But sum word I pronounce as nyghtbouris doys.
Like as in Latyn beyn Grew termys sum,
So me behufyt quhilum or than be dum
Sum bastard Latyin, French or Inglys oyss
Quhar scant was Scottis – I had nane other
  choys.

Great poetry is a union of important meaning and beautifully appropriate sound, so it cannot be put into another speech without great loss, unless the translator compensates for the losses by creating new beauties to replace them. Douglas *gets more poetry out of Virgil than any other translator*, said Ezra Pound, and gets it where Virgil's *Aeneid* is weakest, in its descriptions of bad weather and dreary country. The Scots had more descriptive words for these

MODERN TRANSLATION

Now by your leave, good sirs, I first advise
View my work well before you criticize.
Read more than once. Consider. Give it
thought.
Not in a blink sly poetry is caught,
And yet in truth I took much busy pain,
All that I could, to make it broad and plain,
Keeping no southern, but our language,
Speaking it as I learned it when a page
But not so pure all southern I refuse.
A few words I pronounce as neighbour does.
Just as in Latin are some words of Greek
So I was bound to use (or else not speak)
Some bastard Latin, French or English voice
Where Scots fell short – I had not other choice.

than the Latins, just as the Dutch have more words for dung than other nations, and the Eskimos more words for snow. The *Aeneos* (as Douglas called it) turns heroic classical warriors into Scottish ones, as Henryson turns beasts in Greek and French fables into types of Scottish burghers and clergy.

But the most popular Scottish poem for centuries was by Harry the Minstrel, probably the same maker as the Blind Harry lamented by Dunbar. *The*

Actis and Deidis of the Illustre and Vallyent Campioun Schir William Wallace was one of the first books printed in Scotland around 1508 and went through twenty-three editions before the Union of Parliaments in 1707. Most Scots have always preferred Wallace to Bruce as a national hero. Harry's poem blends historic fact, several very tall tales and intense anti-English feeling. It has Wallace practically conquer England and the English queen's affections before his betrayal and execution, and says

> It was his life, and most part of his food
> To see them shed the burning southrone blood,

them being his followers and *southrone* the south British. Harry's heroic couplets break out at times into verses with more intricate, Chaucerian rhyme schemes than Barbour and Douglas used, some as powerful as the following. It addresses Wallace as he returns to fight for independence after his marriage, not knowing his wife will soon be murdered. It needs no translation if we remember that *lieff* = leave in the first five lines but means 'live' in the last, that *plesance* = pleasure, *loss a gage* = lose a pledge or promise, *erd* = earth, *wer* = war.

Now leiff the myrth, now leiff thi haill
plesance;
Now leiff thi bliss, now leiff thi childis age;
Now leiff thi zouth, now folow thi hard
chance;
Now leiff thi lust, now leiff the mariage;
Now leiff the luff, for thou sall loss a gage
Quilk neuir in erd sall be remedyt agayne,
Folow fortoun, and all hir fers owtrage;
Go leiff in wer, go leiff in cruell payne.

The Wallace has had many reincarnations. In 1722 it was modernised into heroic couplets by William Hamilton and became the most commonly owned book in Scotland next to the bible. Burns read it when a boy and later said, *The story of Wallace poured a Scottish prejudice in my veins which will boil along there till the floodgates of life shut in eternal rest.* In his radical youth Wordsworth thought of writing a new epic on the theme. English chartists drank to Wallace and William Tell as champions of the common man against tyranny. Jane Porter re-wrote it as a best-selling novel in 1810 entitled *The Scottish Chiefs,* which was translated into Russian, German, French then banned as subversive by Napoleon, then Emperor of Europe. *Braveheart,* another novel version, became a successful Hollywood film in

1995 when north Italian separatists used it as propaganda against the Roman parliament. Most Scottish historians have been annoyed and embarrassed by Wallace legends, but have generally failed to give a more truthful, unprejudiced account of him because the documents they most rely on are English state papers. (Scottish state papers before 1650, packed carefully into barrels, were accidentally sunk in the Firth of Forth while being transshipped by Cromwell's agents.) Younger historians now think much of Harry's poem may be cautiously used as a source of information, just as Homer's poem guided Schliemann to the site of Troy when historians had begun doubting that it existed as more than a poetic fantasy.

Last poet in this group is Sir David Lyndsay,

KING HUMANITIE'S PRAYER

Sen Thow has given me dominatioun
And rewll of pepill subject to my cure,
Be I nocht rewlit be counsall and ressoun,
In dignitie I may nocht lang indure.
I grant, my stait my self may nocht assure,
Nor yit conserve mylyfe in sikerness:
Have pitie, Lord, on mee, Thy creature,
Supportand me in all my business.

tutor to infant James V and later that king's chief courtier and diplomat. Throughout the reformation his verse was as popular as Blind Harry's because it attacked clerical corruption. Most of it now seems dull and pedantic when compared with his satire on *The Thrie Estates of Scotland.* Here the verse is clashed into vitality by being put in the mouths of brisk, determined folk representing every social class from pauper to king. It is an astonishing play to have been written by a royal servant. True, the player king is *King Humanity*, a kind of Everyman, but he is also an obviously Scottish king whose main vice is sexual indulgence, the commonest failing among kings in every age.

Young *King Humanity* begins by praying to God and Jesus to help him do his important job well.

THE MODERN TRANSLATION

Since you have given me domination
And rule of people subject to my cure,
If I'm not ruled by good advice and reason
In dignity I may not long endure.
I grant, my state my self cannot make sure,
Nor yet preserve my life in certainness.
Have pity, Lord, on me, Your creature,
Supporting me in all my busy-ness.

At which a cheerful servant, *Wantonness* (which means loose living), persuades him to stop brooding and enjoy life and embrace the lady *Sensuality*. The king embraces her while *Wantonness* admits more vices who start corrupting *The Three Estates* – nobility, clergy and prosperous townsmen. The vices disguise themselves as virtues and jail the real virtues.

Flattery, dressed as a friar *Devotion*, has *Verity* (truth) arrested for heresy – she uses a vernacular *New Testament*. Because *Sensuality* now rules all three estates only a shoemaker and tailor welcome *Chastity*: they prefer booze to sex. Their infuriated wives expel her. Behind the farce we see a nation managed by shameless parasites. It is saved by *Divine Correction*, an angel who rebukes the king and orders him to summon *The Three Estates* who march in backward, led by their vices. A church spokesman says they've gone backward for years and enjoy it. *Correction* orders all who have been wronged to tell the king. From the audience a ragged man jumps on stage: John Commonwealth. He tells how the classes employed to help the nation help only themselves. Lyndsay (says J. Keay) *brings first ruler then ruled from guilty chaos into moral order.* His verse is informed by ideas from Langland, Skelton and Erasmus, and while not beautiful is strong and pithy. Says his court jester: *The king? What kind of man is that? Is yon him in the golden hat?*

James V died of cholera when thirty, having given his folk a lasting Court of Session. He left (like his ancestors) an infant heir for his nobles to fight over: Mary, Queen of Scots.

Notes

The Mercat Anthology of Early Scottish Literature, 1375–1707, ed. R.D.S. Jack & P.A.T. Rozendaal, Edinburgh, Mercat Press, 1997.
(This has all the *King's Quair*, and a little of Henryson and Dunbar.)

Canongate Classics no. 88, *The Makars*, ed. J. Tasioulas, Edinburgh, 1999. (This has the complete works of Henryson and Dunbar, with Douglas's *Palis of Honoure*, with notes.)

Canongate Classics no. 106, *The Wallace* by Blind Harry, edited and introduced by Anne McKim, 2002.

Blind Harry's Wallace translated by William Hamilton of Gilbertfield, introduced by Elspeth King, Edinburgh, Luath Press, 1998.

Canongate Classics no. 18, *Ane Satyre of the Thrie Estaitis* by Sir David Lindsay, edited and introduced by Roderick Lyall, 1989.

CHAPTER FOUR

Destruction and Reform, Ballads and Songs

GOOD WRITERS OFTEN come in clusters, partly because a public is eager for them, partly because each is stimulated by the others' activity. Nearly two centuries divide the great works of Chaucer's age from the equally great works of Shakespeare, and a similar gap divides the makers of the last chapter from a later group called The Enlightenment. Good writing never stopped completely, of course. Despite England's foreign and civil wars, despite headsmen's axes and heretics' bonfires, Arthurian fables were printed, More's *Utopia,* Skelton's satires, Wyatt's lyrics, a grand vernacular bible and prayerbook. But before England's political turbulence calmed enough to allow a new, wider growth of good writing, Scotland was upset in ways that left hardly anyone peace to make a large, generous, satisfying work.

First came another English invasion with as bad a destruction of towns, abbeys and monastic libraries as any ordered by Edward, Hammer of the

Scots. Then came civil wars with greedy noblemen ruling on behalf of an infant queen living in Paris. Some were Protestants bribed by England, some Catholics bribed by France. Many took money from both sides while grabbing all the Church property they could. The worst paid and educated clergy had always been parish priests. These now mainly survived with the help of Calvinist laymen who urged the destruction of Catholic writings, music, statuary and ornament, so the vandalism begun by Henry VIII's armies was completed by local enthusiasts. The short reign of Queen Mary did not bring peace. She too left an infant heir who great landowners struggled to control. He grew up cowardly but shrewd, and had begun getting his nation into something like peaceful order when Elizabeth of England died and he became FIRST RULING MONARCH OF ALL BRITAIN – in London, of course. This made the Scots parliament impotent. It had never been strong.

I will not try to summarise the upheavals provoked by James's sons and grandsons, the strife between Church and State, Scots and English, parliament and nobility which resulted in the last Stuart king's expulsion from Britain in 1688. For nearly twenty years after that the Scots did get a parliament that represented many of them, but in

1707 this was abolished through a financial deal between the richest families of both realms. Between *The Three Estates* and that date much anti-English, anti-Catholic and anti-Protestant polemic was published, also Knox's *History of the Reformation* and *Confession of Faith*, many strongly worded sermons, memoirs and histories of the Covenanters. Most of this writing is wearisome because the authors are sure all who disagree with them are wicked or stupid. This is even true of George Buchanan, who wrote mostly in Latin, and was an internationally famous poet, historian and advocate of peoples' right to replace bad rulers. He was Queen Mary's tutor and loyal supporter until her husband Darnley was murdered. She may have been a party to the crime for she quickly married the man most suspected of it, but when denouncing her afterward Buchanan deliberately lied. That was commonplace. Scotland was then in the anarchic state of Germany and much of France. England survived religious conflicts more peacefully because most of the English changed their form of worship as often as their king or queen wanted. The Scots could not do it so readily because after 1603 their kings and queens were foreign to them.

So the pleasantest vernacular writing to survive from late 16th- and all 17th-century lowland

Scotland are, if we omit folk ballads, enough scattered poems to fill a wee book, and Sir Thomas Urquhart of Cromarty's translation of Rabelais' *Gargantua and Pantagruel.* The latter is rightly thought the best translation of this work into English, not because the text is closest to the original – it is almost a third longer – but because it seems closest to how Rabelais would have written had he not been French. Rabelais enjoyed the fun of heaping nouns and adjectives into long lists mixing rude with polite, slang with outlandish scholarship. Urquhart enlarged these lists by coining new words (as Gavin Douglas did) out of *bastard Latin, French and English,* also Greek. Urquhart's Greek was got from dictionaries instead of Homer, but he loved dictionaries. Among Scots writers only Hugh MacDiarmid had a better appetite for them.

Meanwhile the Catholic and Protestant Gaels were as active in British politics as the lowlanders. From 1645 onward Iain Lom, bard of the MacDonald clan, celebrated battle with the Campbells, who were usually allies of the London government. His poetry laments, denounces, satirises the battle of Killiekrankie, the 1788 revolution, the massacre of Glencoe and a Union of Parliaments which, like most others in Scotland, he saw as having been achieved by bribery.

After 1788 Scots who felt their culture threatened by London rule strove to preserve it by collections of songs and ballads that had evolved for centuries but seldom been printed. There are two theories about the origins of folk poetry, one believed by Burns, the other by Walter Scott, both of whom made Scotland's greatest collections. Bred as a farmer, Burns thought the verses he recorded were composed by commoners like himself, with singers and reciters of later ages making such changes and improvements as their talents allowed. Scott was a lawyer when professional success depended on patronage and employment by the nobility. He believed all the great lowland ballads were first composed for the nobility by professional minstrels like the bards of the highland chiefs, who vanished with Protestant reform and the Union of Crowns. However composed, Scots folk poetry is a surprisingly large body of great work. A detour into England may explain why the larger nation produced less.

Rudyard Kipling's *Barrack Room Ballads* were written to celebrate the thoughts and feelings of English private soldiers, who were not (thought Kipling) properly respected by the prospering classes and rulers of an empire the soldiers maintained. To indicate their Cockney dialect (which was not his own) he omitted initial aitches, writing *ome* instead of *home*. Orwell said this spoiled the beauty of good lines and that *Kipling ought to have known better . . . In the ancient ballads the lord and peasant speak the same language*. But in England they hardly ever did. Before the mid-20th century there were only two short periods when sons of farmers and tradesmen attended Oxford and Cambridge: Chaucer and Shakespeare's times. By the 18th century highly literate people thought common speech a sign of social inferiority, especially in writing. The clear brisk prose of Swift and Defoe gave way to Addison and Dr Johnson's heavier, more Latinate prose. Fashionable folk so larded their speech with French that Johnson feared English might become a French dialect, yet he left English technical words out of his dictionary because he thought polite folk would not need them, though Shakespeare had used them. While sure that Shakespeare and Homer were greater than all later writers, he believed his nation was now politer, and that a writer's main task was to keep it so. He thought folk ballads negligible because they pleased the rude and uneducated, a fashionable attitude that depressed English song. Compare these two lyrics. The English one has a chorus after each couplet: *Downe a downe, hay downe, hay downe, With a downe derrie, derrie downe:* which I omit.

THE TWA CORBIES

As I was walking all alane,
  I heard twa corbies making a mane;
The tane unto the t'other say
  'Where sall we gang and dine today?'

'In behint yon auld fail dyke.
  I wot there lies a new-slain knight;
And naebody kens that he lies there,
  But his hawk, his hound, and his lady fair.

'His hound is to the hunting gane,
  His hawk, to fetch the wild-fowl hame,
His lady's ta'en another mate,
  So we may mak our dinner sweet.

'Ye'll sit on his white hause-bane,
  And I'll pike out his bonny blue een.
Wi' ae lock o' his gowden hair,
  We'll theek our nest when it grows bare.

THE TWO RAVENS

There were two ravens sat on a tree,
They were as black as they might be,

The one of them said to his mate,
'Where shall we our breakfast take?'

'Downe in yonder green field,
There lies a knight slain under his shield.

'His hounds they lie down at his feete,
So well they can their master keepe.

'His haukes they flie so eagerly,
There's no fowl dare him come nie.'

Downe there comes a fallow doe,
As great with yong as she might goe.

She lift up his bloudy hed,
And kist his wounds that were so red.

She got him up upon her backe,
And carried him to earthen lake.

'Mony a one for him makes mane,
  But nane sall ken where he is gane;
O'er his white banes, when they are bare,
  The wind sall blaw for evermair.'

In both poems birds speak for a greedy, uncaring part of the universe that will swallow us all one day, and if we value poetry for its truth the English poem is as true as the Scottish. It is not unlikely that a loyal hawk and hound will protect their master's corpse, or that a loving mistress, heavy with his child, hurts herself giving him Christian burial where his enemies refuse it and dies by the effort. The prayer at the end indicates that not every gentleman can have such loyalty. The ravens vanish from this story when *the fallow doe*, the knight's mistress appears. The last two lines are a Christian conclusion because they pray hopefully for every man, while the chorus makes it a thoroughly social poem.

The Twa Corbies starts with the human voice of a lone traveller who hears a raven question its mate in the first verse. The rest are the reply which suggest *a new slain knight* has been killed by his mistress's lover and that no loyalty or regard for him remain. There is a gloating note in the version of how the knight's body will be used, but by having us identify

She buried him before the prime,
She was dead herselfe ere even-song time.

God send every gentleman
Such hauks, such hounds, and such a leman.

with the non-human, carnivorous part of nature we get a bracing sense of having faced the worst – faced it with pleasure, for there is a grand music in the alternation of long aw and ay sounds that exactly fits the activities described, if the poem is said with the right accent. The title in itself sounds like cawing, and the last couplet like the bluster of wind over a very barren heath. But while seeming pitiless it is not finally anti-human. The last couplet is a lament for all who know we must die and eventually be forgotten.

FINE FLOWERS IN THE VALLEY

She sat down below a thorn,
  Fine flowers in the valley
And there she has her sweet babe born.
  And the green leaves they grow rarely

'Smile na sae sweet, my bonie babe,'
  Fine flowers in the valley

'And ye smile sae sweet, ye'll smile me dead.'
  And the green leaves they grow rarely

She's taen out her little pen-knife,
  Fine flowers in the valley
And twinnd the sweet babe o its life.
  And the green leaves they grow rarely

She's howket a grave by the light o the moon,
  Fine flowers in the valley
And there she's buried her sweet babe in.
  And the green leaves they grow rarely

As she was going to the church,
  Fine flowers in the valley
She saw a sweet babe in the porch.
  And the green leaves they grow rarely

'O sweet babe, and thou were mine,'
  Fine flowers in the valley
'I wad cleed thee in the silk so fine.'
  And the green leaves they grow rarely

'O mother dear, when I was thine,'
  Fine flowers in the valley
'You did na prove to me sae kind.'
  And the green leaves they grow rarely

The use of the refrain here shows the highest art by putting the friendless woman, lonely birth-pangs, pity for the babe, etc. in a frame of constantly fresh, bright, spring-like nature. And note the absence of moralising.

There are at least sixty great ballads, mostly much longer than these. Some, like *Sir Patrick Spens, The Battle of Otterburn*, and *Johnnie Armstrong* are based on historic events. Others (*The Wife of Usher's Well, The Demon Lover, Clerk Saunders*) are tales of the supernatural – all work of the pithiest possible account about what folk do and say and what follows. Some end happily but none commit the common literary crime of telling us what to think or feel about what they describe. The ballads dating from old Catholic times must have been altered by those who sang or chanted them through two troubled centuries of Reformation, but none refer much to Christianity. The speaking apparition of a dead baby in a church porch, summoned there by a mother's guilty conscience, is typical of religious experience in these poems. They never suggest that faith helps or consoles. The *Lyke Wake Dirge* begs Christ to receive our soul when we die, but the only comfort it offers is that we will not be pricked and burned *to the bare bane* if we have given shoes, meat and drink to the poor while living. The Demon

Lover's woman has a brief glimpse of heaven from a sailing ship.

> 'O what are those hills, those pleasant hills
> The sun shines sweetly on?'
> 'Those are the hills o' Heaven,' he said
> 'Where you will never win.'
>
> 'And whaten a mountain is thon,' she cried,
> 'So dreary wi' frost and snow?'
> 'Thon is the mountain o' Hell,' he said,
> 'Whaur you and I will go.'

The drowned sons of *The Wife of Usher's Well* return to their mother's house *in earthly flesh and blood.* Her witchcraft has made God let them out of heaven for one night only. The last verse suggests that they regret having to return, that their earthly home is friendlier.

> 'Fare ye weel, my mither dear!
> Fareweel to barn and byre!
> And fare ye weel, the bonny lass,
> That kindles my mither's fire.'

Some ballads suggest wild hilarity over a cattle raid, prison raid or successful acts of bloody mayhem –

And he has burned the dales o' Tyne
And part of Bambrough-shire,
And three tall towers on Roxburgh Fells,
He left them all on fire.

A different amusement is found in how little our wishes correspond to facts. Here are ambassadors returning from Norway on a ship that has sprung an unmendable leak.

O laith, laith were oor guid Scots lairds
To wet their cork-heeled shoon,
But lang afore the play was played
They wet their hats aboon.

This willingness to accept the worst as an unavoidable part of life is the essence of tragedy.

It also partly explains why, when the Catholic faith failed in Britain, many Scots united to make the harshest of all Protestant faiths, Calvinism, their national religion. No other European nation did that. Calvinism insisted that all Christians should know the bible, so John Knox had striven to turn clergy into schoolmasters who made sure every child in their parish learned to read. The scheme was backed by a bishop James VI forced upon Scotland. It brought greater literacy and the

King James bible to many working-class homes. That book, translation by William Tyndal, was mainly based on the early 16th century and the grave music of its verses influenced Scots speech and writing long after the bible ceased to be fashionable among the politer English.

Notes

The Gargantua and Pantagruel of Rabelais, translated by Sir Thomas Urquhart, ed. David Campbell, London, Everyman's Library, 1994.
Canongate Classic no. 55, *Scottish Ballads* edited and introduced by Emily Lyle, 1994.

CHAPTER FIVE

Eighteenth-century Writers Away and at Home

JAMES BOSWELL CAME to London in search of a brilliant career because he felt (and said so in his diary) that the Act of Union had reduced Scotland to the status of a province. He failed to get a commission in a fashionable regiment, failed to become a brilliant lawyer at the English bar, but devotion to Dr Johnson brought him into a club with Garrick, Goldsmith, Edmund Burke and Joshua Reynolds. It also let him write the best accounts of Johnson's life and character ever published, based on diaries kept when visiting or travelling with Johnson. He was thought nothing but Johnson's biographer before 1950 when diaries he had never meant for publication appeared. They had been found in an Irish castle and proved him as great a diarist as Pepys. He describes dealings with actresses, prostitutes and the resulting pox as frankly as his encounters with Voltaire, Rousseau and Rousseau's mistress.

Boswell was one of several Scots who did well in the south by successfully Englishing themselves. For nearly a century James Thomson was Scotland's most famous British poet. Admirers believed that what Alexander Pope did for polite society Thomson did for the world of nature. In big Miltonic sentences of blank verse he evoked weather and landscapes, often with generalised peasants doing seasonal jobs. They do not convince like the verse of Henryson and Douglas because this is how he writes:

> Come, gentle Spring, ethereal mildness, come;
> And from the bosom of yon dropping cloud,
> While music wakes around, veiled in a shower
> Of shadowing roses, on our plains descend.
>
> O Hartford, fitted or to shine in courts
> With unaffected grace, or walk the plain
> With innocence and meditation joined
> In soft assemblage, listen to my song.

He is addressing the Countess of Hartford. His main political writing was patriotic stage plays, one containing the song *Rule Britannia*! His noble patrons made him Surveyor General of the Leeward Isles; a title and regular salary without a job attached to it.

James MacPherson, most famous of all Scots authors in those days, was a young school-teacher from Inverness who knew professors and clergy connected with the Advocates Library in Edinburgh, which was then collecting ancient and historic documents that have made it into the National Library of Scotland. Though Gaelic had been Scotland's main language the library's officials and friends could neither read nor speak it, so MacPherson gave them what he called translations of ancient Gaelic poetry – fragments of heroic epic he had collected in the highlands. They mentioned heroes who do occur in old Gaelic poems, where they seem as distinctly human as the warriors of Homer. MacPherson's heroes loom dim yet titanic; his lowland friends felt this right for a remote Scottish era and published what he gave. Homer's warriors squabble between battles for possession of loot and captured women. MacPherson's mostly brood or lament, so many polite readers preferred them. He never produced ancient manuscripts so Dr Johnson called the translations fake, but scholars who read Gaelic were then as few as ancient manuscripts so gave MacPherson the benefit of their doubts: especially when his writings brought fame to the nation where they were forged. Goethe praised them. Young Napoleon tried to write something similar in French. You can see why if you compare this specimen with the grammar of Thomson's address to spring and to his countess, for at that time poetic speech in France was as stilted as in England.

> The blue waves of Erin roll in light. The mountains are covered with day. Grey torrents pour their noisy streams. Two Green hills, with aged oaks, surround a narrow plain. The blue course of a stream is there. On its banks stood Cairbar of Atha. His spear supports the king: the red eye of his fear is sad.

Luis Borges said MacPherson sacrificed honesty *to the greater glory of Scotland* and thereby wrote *the first Romantic poem in European literature.* If Romantic means a story in places exotically distant from the author and readers then MacPherson was certainly first in a new movement that included Coleridge, Keats, Tennyson, Poe and Browning. Despite Johnson's contempt he was made Surveyor General of Florida, prospered as a merchant and got buried at his own expense in Westminster Abbey.

Besides Boswell, Tobias Smollett is the main Scots expatriate of that age who can still be read with pleasure. George Orwell called him *Scotland's greatest novelist* because he departed from the English novel's main tradition. This required a good-natured, selfish or foolish hero who can fit easily into fashionable society and, after misadventures, marries and gains a secure unearned income. This was the plot of nearly every successful London stage comedy from the restoration of the monarchy in 1660 to the days of Bernard Shaw. Henry Fielding brought it into the novel from where it spread through a deal of inferior fiction, and nearly spoils the end of Scott's and Dickens's finest works by suggesting that a wedding solves every problem for good people. Fielding tried to promote a cleaner world by writing as if filth and cruelty were departures from a sensible, upper-middle-class, south British norm. Smollett was a doctor who had served in the British navy. His horror of dirt was so 20th-century that some of his contemporaries thought it insane. Laurence Sterne called him *Dr Smellfungus* because Smollett said most inns and fashionable assemblies stank, as did the medicinal wells of Bath where many rich people with running sores immersed together in the same tank of tepid water. Smollett aimed to promote a better society by showing bustling, knockabout Britain as he saw it, which is how Hogarth, the first and greatest truly English painter depicted it. They confirm each other. His main characters are snobs, bullies or rogues and sometimes all three. They fight on the slightest provocation and amuse themselves with casual sex and pitilessly cruel practical jokes. Says Orwell, *By ruling out 'good' motives and showing no respect for human dignity Smollett attains a truthfulness that more serious novels have missed.* The hero of *Roderick Random* is probably the first in British fiction before the coming of AIDS to contract a venereal disease. When touring Europe he runs out of money and earns it by enlisting with a French regiment, eventually fighting his countrymen on a German battlefield. Afterward he fights a duel with a French officer who speaks offensively of England. Britain and France were then the strongest, most belligerent, and (in their own opinions) most civilised nations in the world, and certainly had large armies with the best fire-arms. Until Napoleon lost the battle of Waterloo in 1815 each fought to grab away from the other chunks of Asia, America and Africa; but their wars (unlike religious wars in the previous century, which they thought barbarous) were fought for commercial gain, not for the Kingdom of Heaven, so private citizens broke no laws when they profited by war in ways extreme patriots now might think treasonable. British politicians with shares in arms industries have returned to 18th-century practices, but even today no honourable gentleman will let his nation be *insulted*.

If you have a strong stomach Smollett's novels are amusing guides to what most polite folk then ignored or took for granted, but professors and teachers of English thought novels too popular to be good literature. They thought philosophy was, along with those branches of natural philosophy now called physics and psychology, so gentlemen's libraries were decorated with busts of Shakespeare, Milton, Locke and Isaac Newton.

But by 1750 Newton, Boyle, Hooke and other great founders of the Royal London Society for the Advancement of Natural Knowledge were dead. Oxford and Cambridge colleges had recovered from the intellectual excitements of the previous century and returned to the tradition that knowledge of manual and mechanical works were the business of slaves, serfs and the *lower* middle classes. They taught anatomy, chemistry and botany besides classical literature, theology and mathematics, but teaching was not rigorous. They were mainly social clubs where sons of the noble and prosperous enjoyed themselves by rubbing along together, made contacts that would be useful in later life, and took a degree that let them become Church of England clergy if nothing better offered. Meanwhile industrialists in Birmingham, Manchester and Staffordshire were discovering cheaper, faster, better ways to forge metal, spin thread, weave cloth and fire pottery. They did so while corresponding with scientists in Scots universities.

The bad slump in trade and confidence that caused the 1707 Union of Parliaments had been followed by an astonishing recovery. While Scotland's hereditary lords played party politics in London their land was chiefly managed by lawyers who saw how to increase its value. New methods were found to make farms out of wilderness and money from local deposits of coal and iron. Clydeside ship-owners acquired big plantations and many slaves in the West Indies and America, becoming major importers of sugar, cotton and tobacco. This mainly happened because Scotland, compared with England, combined a generally lower standard of living with a generally higher standard of education. Sons of farmers, builders and shopkeepers attended her universities with young lairds whose income would depend on them. Those not studying to be ministers and lawyers wanted knowledge to make their work more profitable. Glasgow University employed James Watt as a mechanic and James Black as a professor of chemistry. Their conferences enabled Watt to design a steam engine that accelerated industry and transport throughout the world. By using down-to-earth, closely observed facts to prove big theories David Hume, James Hutton, Adam Ferguson and Adam Smith wrote the first books on which modern philosophy, geology, sociology and economics are based. These are still worth reading. Law and mathematics in those days were the only sciences with many hard words needing much study before common sense could grasp them. Political economy has sprouted in ways that would have amazed Adam Smith. He argued that workmen's skill, not an unrestricted money market, made the Wealth of Nations.

To reach as wide a public as possible they wrote words that were common to both Scots and English, but spoke Scots among themselves. So did most lowland Scots, apart from the very rich who sent sons to southern public schools and Oxbridge. In this vernacular idiom Allan Ramsay (wig-maker, librarian, song collector) wrote a pastoral comedy. Robert Fergusson, a lawyer's clerk, wrote satires in it before dying aged twenty-four in a madhouse. Burns called him *My elder brother in misfortune, by far my elder brother in the muse.* This hymn to broad cloth – the finest quality of woven black material – shows why Burns loved him.

BRAID CLAITH

Ye wha are fain to hae your name
Wrote in the bonny book of fame,
Let merit nae pretension claim
To laurel'd wreath,
But hap ye weel, baith back and wame, — wrap, belly
In gude Braid Claith.

He that some ells o' this may fa', — get
An snae-black hat on pow like snaw,
Bids bauld to bear the gree awa' — prize
Wi a'this graith, — stuff
Whan bienly clad wi' shell fu' braw — well, handsome
O' gude Braid Claith.

Waesuck for him wha has nae feck o't! — Alas, amount
For he's a gowk they're sure to geck at, — fool, mock
A chield that ne'er will be respekit
While he draws breath,
Till his four quarters are bedeckit
Wi gude Braid Claith.

On Sabbath-days the barber spark,	
Whan he has done wi' scrapin wark,	
Wi' siller broachie in his sark,	shirt
Gangs trigly, faith!	Goes neatly
Or to the Meadow, or the Park,	
In gude Braid Claith.	
Weel might ye trow, to see them there,	believe
That they to shave your haffits bare,	cheeks
Or curl an' sleek a pickle hair,	lot of
Wou'd be right laith,	loath, unwilling
Whan pacing wi' a gawsy air	stately
In gude Braid Claith.	
If ony mettl'd stirrah green	fellow looks
For favour frae a lady's ein,	
He maunna care for being seen	may not
Before he sheath	
His body in a scabbard clean	
O' gude Braid Claith.	
For, gin he come wi' coat thread-bare,	if
A feg for him she winna care,	fig
But crook her bony mou' fu' sair,	mouth, full/very, sorely

An' scald him baith. — scold
Wooers shou'd ay their travel spare
Without Braid Claith.

Braid Claith lends folk an unco heese, — big lift
Makes mony kail-worms butter fleas, — cabbage
Gies mony a doctor his degrees
For little skaith: — trouble
In short, you may be what you please
Wi' gude Braid Claith.

For though ye had as wise a snoot on
As Shakespeare or Sir Isaac Newton,
Your judgment folk wou'd hae a doubt on,
I'll tak my aith,
Till they cou'd see ye wi' a suit on
O' gude Braid Claith.

Lady Nairne, Lady Anne Lindsay and others wrote tender and funny lyrics in this idiom, lyrics often reprinted as Scots folk songs. Such writing allowed every social class to delight in the poetry of Burns when his first book appeared in 1786.

But a chapter that tells of a phoney Gaelic poet should at least mention two real ones. The following facts are mainly taken from John and Julia Keay's *Encyclopaedia of Scotland.*

Alexander MacDonald (in Gaelic, Alasdair macMhaighstir Alasdair) was related to the chiefs of Islay, studied for law or the church at university (probably Glasgow) and fought for Charles Edward Stewart in the '45 rising. He wrote poems of love and vituperation; descriptions of the seasons suggested by, but superior to, Thomson's *Seasons*; calls to battle; political satire and laments for the destruction of his people's way of life. The *Encyclopaedia* says his work is *an extraordinary blend of exuberance and contemplation. He sees action against a historical and partly philosophical background.* One of his poems, 'Clanranald's Galley', was Englished by Hugh MacDiarmid aided by Sorley MacLean. With great clarity, energy and excitement it evokes the work of each part of a crew taking a ship of the Viking sort to Ireland through a fearful storm. Even in translation the poem appeals to the reader's muscles as much as vision. If we wonder where the poet stands among crewmen he so closely exhorts we find he is in the position of captain, directing and encouraging their efforts. This puts the reader in the same position, giving a sense of partnership with, mastery over, men and a wild North Sea.

Duncan Ban MacIntyre was a highlander who,

like many others, fought *against* Prince Charlie in the 1745 rising. He lived through the massacres and destruction of the clan system that followed and saw fellow Gaels driven by hunger to enlist in the British army, where generals used them as excellent cannon fodder in imperial wars. MacIntyre was gamekeeper on the slopes of Ben Dorain which he loved and described in verse. He was illiterate, his poetry now known because a minister's son at Killin wrote it down. If the music of his Gaelic is as fine as its sense in translation then his verse is among the finest nature poetry in Britain. When seventy-five and too old to be a gamekeeper he joined Edinburgh's city guard, a notably incompetent police force.

Notes

Canongate Classic no. 68: *Journey to the Hebrides* by Samuel Johnson and James Boswell, edited by Ian McGowan, 1996.

The Life of Samuel Johnson by James Boswell.

Roderick Random, *Ferdinand Count Fathom*, *Peregrine Pickle* and *Humphrey Clinker* by Tobias Smollett.

Canongate Classic no. 80: *The Scottish Enlightenment: An Anthology* edited by Alexander Broadie, 1997.

Poems by Allan Ramsay and Robert Fergusson edited and introduced by A.M. Kinghorn and A. Law, Edinburgh and London, Scottish Academic Press, 1974.

Canongate Classic no. 107: *Before Burns: 18th-Century Poetry in Scots* edited and introduced by Christopher MacLachlan, 2002.

CHAPTER SIX

Robert Burns

HIS DAD RENTED a small farm and worked it with his children's help. Such farms were like small self-supporting republics, in constant danger of ruin by bad harvests or bad landlords. At the age of twelve Robert, by toiling to save a harvest in bad weather, got the rheumatic illness that killed him twenty-five years later, but he lived by such farming for most of his life. From his mother and an old farm servant he learned the songs, ballads and stories of that greatest of Scots geniuses, Anon. Later his dad hired a student during university vacations with whom Burns read Shakespeare, Milton, Pope and some French. When his father's death left him head of the family republic he found a social life with the local Freemasons, a semi-secret society of Scots origin where gentry and manual workers met as equals. Burns's democratic views were those of Jean Jacques Rousseau, Blake, Hazlitt, early Coleridge and Wordsworth, also Byron and Shelley who thought a century of rational improvements should end with the abolition of hereditary kings, lords and the hereditary rights they depended on, as the USA had abolished them. His speech and ideas appear in these two opening verses.

TO A MOUSE

On turning her up in her nest with the plough, November 1785.

Wee, sleeket, cowrin, tim'rous beastie, smooth and soft
O, what a panic's in thy breistie!
Thou need na start awa sae hasty,
    Wi' bickering brattle! squeaking hurry
I wad be laith to rin an' chase thee,
    Wi' murdering pattle! stick for breaking clods

I'm truly sorry Man's dominion,
Has broken Nature's social union,
An' justifies that ill opinion,
    Which makes thee startle
At me, thy poor, earth-born companion,
    An fellow mortal.

The first verse uses homely Scots to convey a sympathy that Henryson also showed toward mice and other small people. The apology in the next verse rejects the bible's notion that God has given man dominion over all the beasts of the field and suggests men have seized power like tyrants, instead of living and letting live. Burns is extending the social contract – the idea that men combined in nations to help each other, as they did in families – to embrace all natural life, so uses a bible word with others from modern political philosophy. T.S. Eliot said Burns's language showed the decadence of a great tradition because he used English for large world views, unlike the Scots makers of two centuries before. But their large world-views were scholastic Catholic. Scots culture had passed through Calvinism – which agreed with Catholicism so far as to think the natural world and natural human appetites evil – but people like Hume, Adam Smith and Burns believed that the laws of God and Nature should be the same, and human laws were at fault when they contradicted natural sympathetic feeling. The second verse uses the language of higher education throughout Britain and the USA. Burns resumes his rural diction to describe the mouse's domestic state: and his own.

Thy wee bit housie, too, in ruin!
Its silly wa's the win's are strewin!
An naething, now, to big a new ane, build

O' foggage green! grass crop
An' bleak December's winds ensuin,
Baith snell an' keen! biting

Thou saw the fields laid bare an' waste,
An' weary Winter comin fast,
An' cozie here, beneath the blast,
Thou thought to dwell,
Till crash! The cruel coulter past plough blade
Out thro' thy cell.

That wee bit heap o' leaves an' stibble,
Has cost thee monie a waery nibble!
Now thou's turned out, for a' thy trouble,
But house or hald, without house or stronghold
To thole the Winter's sleety dribble, suffer
An' cranreuch cauld! hoar-frost

But Mousie, thou art no thy lane,
In proving foresight may be vain;
The best-laid schemes o' mice an' men
Gang aft agley, squint, wrong
An' lea'e us nought but grief an' pain,
For promis'd joy!

Still thou art blest, compar'd wi' me!
The present only toucheth thee:
But och! I backward cast my e'e,
On prospects drear!
An' forward, tho' I canna see,
I guess an' fear!

This poem is about homelessness. Burns is not sentimentally humanising the mouse in order to enjoy the luxury of pitying it. Nor need he tell us he was supporting a widowed mother, younger brothers, an illegitimate child in a home that might be wrecked by forces as irresistible as that ploughshare through the mouse's nest.

THE JOLLY BEGGARS

See the smoking bowl before us,
Mark our jovial ragged ring!
Round and round take up the chorus,
And in raptures let us sing,—

What is title, what is treasure,
What is reputation's care?
If we lead a life of pleasure,
'Tis no matter how or where!

With the ready trick and fable
  Round we wander all the day;
And at night in barn or stable
  Hug our doxies on the hay.

Does the train-attended carriage
  Thro' the country lighter rove?
Does the sober bed of Marriage
  Witness brighter scenes of love?

Life is all a variorum,
  We regard not how it goes;
Let them cant about decorum,
  Who have character to lose.

Here's to budgets, bags and wallets!
  Here's to all the wandering train!
Here's our ragged Brats and Callets!
  One and all, cry out, – 'AMEN'!

A fig for those by law protected!
  Liberty's a glorious feast!
Courts for Cowards were erected,
  Churches built to please the Priest!

Yet his *Jolly Beggars* cantata shows destitution as cheerily as possible. The soloists are tramps who have pawned their spare clothes to get drunk in an Ayrshire pub: an old soldier who lost an arm and leg in battle; an army whore who now has only him; a clownish idiot; an old female pickpocket; a wandering fiddler; a tinker. These verses are from their final chorus. Burns felt love not only created life but made it worth living, whether in brief encounters, marriage or friendship. Only love of power and money did not please him, so he wrote more poems about other sorts of love than any other poet. He called loving kindness *a carnal inclination* – a gift of the body. Those whose religion made them feel superior to it he exposed as comic hypocrites in *The Holy Fair*, *Holy Willie's Prayer*, and *The Kirk's Alarm*. Most great love poems, including Shakespeare's and Donne's and the Cavalier poets, show only the writers' feelings for the loved one and seldom speak in a woman's voice. They conjure up so little sense of a surrounding society that, apart from an occasional rival for the beloved woman the couple might be living on a desert island. The only exception I can think of is Lovelace's *To Jocasta*, where the lover is departing to a war. Burns's shortest love songs refer to surrounding communities and about half are in the voices of women. Here a young woman plays with her handsome wooer like an angler playing a fish. His attentions to cousin Bess may mean he has played as cunningly too.

THE BRAW WOOER

Last May, a braw wooer cam doun	fine, came
the lang glen,	long
And sair wi' his love he did	sore
deave me;	pester
I said, there was naething I hated	
like men —	
The deuce gae wi'm, to believe me,	
believe me,	
The deuce gae wi'm to believe me.	go with him
He spake o' the darts in my bonie	spoke
black e'en,	eyes
And vow'd for my love he was dyin;	
I said, he might die when he liket for	
Jean —	
The Lord forgie me for lyin,	forgive
for lyin,	
The Lord forgie me for lyin!	
A weel-stocket mailen, himsel	well-stocked
for the laird,	farm
And marriage aff-hand, were his	off-
proffers;	proposals

I never loot on that I kenn'd it, or car'd;	let, knew
But I thought I might hae waur offers, waur offers,	have worse
But I thought I might hae waur offers.	
But what wad ye think? In a fortnight or less,	would
The Deil tak his taste to gae near her!	go
He up the lang loan to my black cousin, Bess!	long lane
Guess ye how, the jad! I could bear her, could bear her,	hussy
Guess ye how, the jad! I could bear her.	
But a' the niest week, as I fretted wi' care,	next
I gaed to the tryste o' Dalgarnock;	fair for hiring farm servants
And wha but my fine fickle lover was there,	who
I glowr'd as I'd seen a warlock, a warlock,	scowled; a male witch
I glowr'd as I'd seen a warlock.	

But owre my left shouther I gae him a blink,
Lest neibours might say I was saucy;
My wooer he caper'd as he'd been in drink,
And vow'd I was his dear lassie, dear lassie,
And vow'd I was his dear lassie.

I spier'd for my cousin fu' couthy and sweet, — asked, politely
Gin she had recover'd her hearin, — if
And how her new shoon fit her auld schachl't feet, — twisted
But heavens! how he fell a swearin, a swearin,
But heavens! how he fell a swearin.

He beggèd for a gudesake, I wad be his wife,
Or else I wad kill him wi' sorrow;
So e'en to preserve the poor body in life, — even
I think I maun wed him to-morrow, to-morrow;
I think I maun wed him to-morrow.

RATTLIN, ROARIN WILLIE

O Rattlin, roarin Willie,
O he held to the fair,
An' for to sell his fiddle
And buy some other ware; — goods

But parting wi' his fiddle,
The saut tear blin't his e'e; — salt, blinded, eye
And Rattlin, roarin Willie,
Ye're welcome hame to me. — home

O Willie, come sell your fiddle,
O, sell your fiddle sae fine;
O Willie, come sell your fiddle,
And buy a pint o' wine;
If I should sell my fiddle,
The warld would think I was mad, — world
For mony a rantin day — many, jovial
My fiddle and I hae had.

As I cam by Crochallan
I cannily keekit ben, — craftily peeked in
Rattlin, roarin Willie
Was sitting at yon boord-en', — board-end/ top of table
Sitting at yon boord-en',
And amang guid companie;
Rattlin, roarin Willie,
Ye're welcome hame to me!

In the last six years of his short life Burns left the drudgery of farming for that of itinerant exciseman. He was efficient, got promoted, but was threatened with dismissal for supporting parliamentary reform and the French Revolution. With no time to concentrate on long, sustained poems he wrote and collected lyrics for traditional fiddle tunes, giving over two hundred of these to publishers and refusing payment because he said they belonged to the Scots people. The harmony between himself and his community appears in this poem.

The first two verses are by the great Anon. Burns wrote the last, which portrays a lawyer friend, William Dunbar, who presided at the Crochallan drinking club. Note the many voices in this and how they merge into a perfect whole. The first voice describes a fellow (whose name suggests he is no family man) going to trade his fiddle for something more needed: is it fuel or food? It halts him close up at a moment of surprising grief, and the teller's voice becomes that of a loving wife welcoming him home with or without fiddle. Half the next verse is the voice of a sneaking tempter, the second half Willie's mournful reply as he still hesitates over the sale. Then the outcome: Willie without fiddle happily presiding in a drinking den, spied there by the wife who will *still* welcome him home. The community of voices linking fair (meaning market) with public house and home has been made in a way described by Joyce in *A Portrait of the Artist as a Young Man:*

> The simplest epical form is seen emerging out of lyrical literature when . . . the personality of the artist passes into the narration itself, flowing round and round the persons and the action like a vital sea. This progress you will see easily in that old English ballad 'Turpin Hero', which begins in the first person and ends in the third person . . . The personality of the artist, at first a cry or a cadence or a mood and then a fluid and lambent narrative, finally refines itself out of existence.

An ingredient of Burns's society that he refined out of sight in his poetry, though not out of its construction, was intellectual enquiry. Another friend of Burns in the Crochalan Club in Edinburgh was William Smellie, printer to the university, first translator of Buffon's zoo-ology into English, main devisor and first Editor of the *Encyclopaedia Britannica*, also publisher of Burns's poems. Smellie, like Burns, kept seeing far less qualified folk than himself promoted to superior appointments because they inherited estates so had political influence. It was noticed that Burns was quite at ease among gentry, but never identified with them in verse, though his self-portrait poems describe other kinds of men: the kindly, careworn ploughman in *To a Mouse*;

heartless seducer in *Rob Mossgiel*; grateful lover in *Corn Riggs*; grimly independent family man in *I Hae a Wife o' my Ain*; a clumsy rustic comically over-awed by nobility in *On Dining with Lord Daer*; and in *A Man's a Man for A' That*, a democrat who believes honesty and common sense will one day establish social equality over all the earth. The last was certainly his political faith.

In 1999 promoters of a revived Scots parliament chose the last song as a national anthem. It was sung at the state opening before the queen, lords and commons. At a more private banquet for the main dignitaries afterwards it was sung again, with the verses mocking royalty and aristocracy omitted.

Burns is still in advance of his nation.

Notes

Burns's poems can be got cheaply in many other editions, secondhand and modern. I suggest that you hear them sung in recordings that use the original tunes. Two good collections exist:

The Songs of Robert Burns are in six tapes issued by Greentrax Records, Edinburgh, sung by the folk singer Jean Redpath. The orchestral accompaniments by Serge Hovey are beautiful and appropriate, except in a few songs like *I'm O'er Young to Marry Yet*, in which they add an eerily haunting tone to carefree words.

Robert Burns, The Complete Songs issued by Linn Products Limited, Eaglesham, Glasgow, are on compact discs compiled and introduced by Doctor Fred Freeman in association with The Burns Federation. There are several singers, sometimes unaccompanied, sometimes with simple guitar accompaniments.

Music lovers should savour the different qualities of both collections.

Canongate Classic no. 104, *The Canongate Burns*, introduced and edited by Andrew Noble and Patrick Scott Hogg, 2001.

CHAPTER SEVEN

Scott. Hogg. Galt

LOWLAND FOLK IN early 19th-century Scotland had confidence in both their international importance and local culture. Their philosophers, scientists, engineers, doctors were valued abroad. Edinburgh was a publishing centre from which the *Encyclopaedia Britannica* and the three most influential literary journals in Britain were distributed to England and the USA. The popularity of Scots songs and Burns's poetry throughout the English-speaking world meant that readers of English everywhere understood common Scots speech, so Galt said Scots authors were lucky to possess *the whole range of the English language, as well as their own, by which they enjoy an unusually rich vocabulary.* And the writers heading this chapter wrote out of an unusually wide social experience.

As a sick little boy Scott was nursed to health on his grandad's farm among shepherds whose talk and ballads were about cattle raids, ancient wars, Covenanters and Jacobite risings. This was his first layer of education and gave the subjects of his best novels. Later came a huge reading of histories and romances – Froissart, Shakespeare, Goethe – and legal study in the Advocates' Library among historic documents and decrees in which Scottish folk heroes were named as brigands and rebels. He visited the highlands and was fascinated by the culture of the Gaelic chieftains while helping them evict their tenants. All this enabled him to create a new literary form – novels in which believable fictional people have dealings with the fictional dead amid a host of folk from all social ranks whom history never mentions: peasants, tradesmen, private soldiers and tramps.

The best of these novels are set in Scotland and have working-class characters speaking in the various idioms of their employments. The author's narrative and the voice of his heroes is in posh English, the heroes of the earliest being English gentry visiting Scotland on military or legal business that involves them in rebellion and civil wars. These heroes are not heroic but good-natured, easily misled young men any reader can identify with because they have no deep religious or political faith. They attach to one side or its opposite through the accidents of their social class, family connections, or a meeting with a stranger. Scott called the hero of his first novel Waverley for the same reason Evelyn Waugh called his first hero Pennyfeather: both are lightweights, struggling to survive while wavering from place to place as events push them. Scott's view of history is Tolstoy's. Scott was a Tory but Marx thought him the first novelist to be realistic about political conflict.

In the following extract Waverley has stopped at a smithy, his horse having lost a shoe. He is fleeing from the highlands in haste to join the English army, for Prince Charles Edward Stuart has landed. The smith, however, is mending flintlock pistols for local Calvinist Whigs also alarmed by the news. The smith's wife hates such folk. She has been rebuked in the kirk for sexual misconduct; some of them must have informed on her; she gladly mistakes Waverley for a Jacobite Tory. Scott enriches her speech with fragments of song Burns had collected. The village senator puts a resounding bible phrase before rhyming off seven Christian creeds thought heresies by the Church of Scotland.

> Ere Waverley could ask particulars, a strong, large-boned, hard-featured woman about forty, dressed as if her clothes had been flung on with a pitch-fork, her cheeks flushed with a scarlet red where they were not smutted with soot and lamp-black, jostled through the

crowd, and, brandishing high a child of two years old, which she danced in her arms, without regard to its screams of terror, sang forth, with all her might: 'Charlie is my darling, my darling, my darling, Charlie is my darling, The young Chevalier!'

'D'ye hear what's come ower ye now,' continued the virago, 'ye whingeing Whig carles? D'ye hear wha's coming to cow yer cracks? "Little wot ye wha's coming, Little wot ye wha's coming, A' the wild Macraws are coming."'

The Vulcan of Cairnvreckan, who acknowledged his Venus in this exulting Bacchante, regarded her with a grim and ire-foreboding coutenance, while some of the senators of the village hastened to interpose. 'Whisht, gudewife; is this a time, or is this a day, to be singing your ranting fule sangs in? – a time when the wine of wrath is poured out without mixture in the cup of indignation, and a day when the land should give testimony against popery, and prelacy, and quakerism, and independency, and supremacy, and erastianism, and antinomianism, and a' the errors of the Church?'

'And that's a' your Whiggery,' re-echoed the Jacobite heroine; 'that's a' your Whiggery, and your presbytery, ye cut-lugged, graning carles! What d'ye think the lads wi' the kilts will care for yer synods and yer presbyteries, and yer buttock-mail, and yer stool o' repentance? Vengeance on the black face o't! Mony an honester woman's been set upon it than streeks doon beside ony Whig in the country. I mysell' –

Here John Mucklewrath, who dreaded her entering upon a detail of personal experience, interposed his matrimonial authority. 'Gae hame and be d—— (that I should say sae), and put on the sowens for supper.'

'And you, ye doil'd dotard,' replied his gentle helpmate, her wrath, which had hitherto wandered abroad over the whole Assembly, being at once and violently impelled into its natural channel, '*ye* stand there hammering dog-heads for fules that will never snap them at a Highlandman, instead of earning bread for your family, and shoeing this winsome young gentleman's horse that's just come frae the north! I'se warrant him name of your whingeing King George folk, but a gallant Gordon, at the least o' him.'

The eyes of the assembly were now turned upon Waverley, who took the opportunity to beg the smith to shoe his guide's horse with all speed, as he wished to proceed on his journey; for he had heard enough to make him sensible that there would be danger in delaying long in this place. The smith's eyes rested on him with a look of displeasure and suspicion, not lessened by the eagerness with which his wife enforced Waverley's mandate. 'D'ye hear what the weel-favoured young gentleman says, ye drunken ne'er-do-good?'

'And what may your name be, sir?' quoth Mucklewrath.

'It is of no consequence to you, my friend, provided I pay your labour.'

'But it may be of consequence to the state, sir,' replied an old farmer, smelling strongly of whisky and peat smoke; 'and I doubt we maun delay your journey till you have seen the Laird.'

'You certainly,' said Waverley haughtily, 'will find it both difficult and dangerous to detain me, unless you can produce some proper authority.'

There was a pause and a whisper among the crowd – 'Secretary Murray,' 'Lord Lewis Gordon;' 'Maybe the Chevalier himsell!' Such were the surmises that passed hurriedly among them, and there was obviously an increased disposition to resist Waverley's departure. He attempted to argue mildly with them, but his voluntary ally, Mrs Mucklewrath, broke in upon and drowned his expostulations, taking his part with an abusive violence, which was all set down to Edward's account by those on whom it was bestowed. '*Ye'll* stop ony gentleman that's the Prince's freend?' for she too, though with other feelings, had adopted the general opinion respecting Waverley. 'I daur ye to touch him,' spreading abroad her long and muscular fingers, garnished with claws which a vulture might have envied. 'I'll set my ten commandments in the face o' the first loon that lays a finger on him.'

'Gae hame, gudewife,' quoth the farmer aforesaid; 'it wad better set you to be nursing the gudeman's bairns than to be deaving us here.'

'*His* bairns!' retorted the Amazon, regarding her husband with a grin of ineffable contempt – '*His* bairns!

O gin ye were dead, gudeman,
  And a green turf on your head, gudeman!
Then I wad ware my widowhood
  Upon a ranting Highlandman.'

This canticle, which excited a suppressed titter among the younger part of the audience, totally overcame the patience of the taunted man of the anvil. 'Deil be in me, but I'll put this het gad down her throat!' cried he, in an ecstasy of wrath, snatching a bar from the forge; and he might have executed his threat had he not been withheld by a part of the mob, while the rest endeavoured to force the termagant out of his presence.

His novels were attacked by late 20th-century critics for two reasons, one unfair, one right. He has been charged with avoiding the political problems of his day by escaping into the past. If so, *Vanity*

Fair, The Scarlet Letter, War and Peace are also escapist fiction, which no good critic believes. He has been charged with poor artistry, melodrama, clumsy plotting. Yes, even his best books have all three at times. The plot of *Waverley* hinges on the hero being imprisoned by an unseen enemy while Jacobites defeat the Scottish Hanoverians. The enemy and his unconvincing motives are only given in the last chapter. Scott thought novel writing a well-paid job, not a fine art, so when imagination failed he never paused to let it recover but used an unlikely coincidence or theatrical cliché to keep the story going. Interesting, believable folk are suddenly posturing against what seem crudely painted backdrops. He published twenty-six novels in fifteen years with more and more exotic settings, less and less believable characters, so nothing he wrote can be swallowed uncritically. But when writing at his best in books like *Heart of Midlothian* and *Old Mortality* he inspired Pushkin, Gogol, Manzoni and Balzac, the last of whom said he wanted to do for modern life what Scott had done for the past: that is, to show all the kinds of people whose lives made a nation. He inspired historians like Guizot and Michelet. *He taught us all*, said Carlyle, *that the past is filled by living men, not by protocols, state papers, controversies and abstractions of men.* Even what now seem his least convincing, most theatrical novels inspired painting by Delacroix, opera by Donizetti.

James Hogg, like Burns, was a tenant farmer's son, but a ruined one. His mother's store of song and story was his first training in poetry and fiction. He taught himself reading and writing in spare moments while working as a shepherd in Ettrick. When Scott raided the district in search of old ballads Hogg provided some. Edinburgh journals began printing his tales and poetry so he flitted there, tried to live by writing, started a small magazine of his own. It failed but he had become famous now and was allowed an easier life than Burns by the Duke of Buccleuch, who gave him a rent-free farm. From this secure base he wrote *The Confessions of a Justified Sinner*, the most perfectly shaped and wonderful of Scottish novels. Half seems a historical third-person narrative, half a confessional autobiography ending in diary notes, and an account of how Edinburgh gentry found the confession in the moorland grave of a Calvinist madman who committed suicide in the last days of the old Scots parliament. It tells how the Calvinist, ugly and cowardly son of a hearty old laird kills and inherits the lands of his handsome, sociable older brother. Through the book glides a being able to take the exact appearance of any other character –

the devil, of course. Great 18th-century writers mostly avoided talk of God and Devil because even Christians like Addison, Pope and Dr Johnson knew that for centuries the most Devilish atrocities had been done by Christians in God's name; but starting with Goethe's *Faust* 19th-century fiction was infested by folk getting power or property through deals with evil agencies: miraculous agencies in the case of Frankenstein, Dr Jekyll, Trilby and Dorian Gray, but usually by plainer methods. In *Great Expectations* Pip prospers and is corrupted by a criminal's generosity. Balzac's most brilliant heroes prosper by theft, hypocrisy, homosexual prostitution and seducing married women. They aren't punished for it. In moral Britain half the Sherlock Holmes stories are about respected citizens having to pay for wealth they got by a crime committed long ago in the Colonies, India or at sea. Hogg makes us pity his poor wretched sinner because we would have grown as bad if taught to fear hellfire from our earliest days in a family whose members hated each other. Only Gogol and Dostoevsky have led us into such sympathy with unpleasant people. André Gide brought the book to public attention in the late 1940s after a century of neglect. He thought its one weakness was the shape-shifting fiend's visibility to folk in the first part of the book: if kept to the last he could have been accepted as a lunatic's delusion. But this versatile devil is a bad part of everyone, so known to more than murderers. In the first part devilish agencies act on several folk by different means: optical illusion, hallucination, group hysteria and (worst of all) amnesia, but the fiend's smartest trick is to kill someone using another man's appearance.

Hogg also wrote *The Three Perils of Man: War, Women and Witchcraft*, a messy plum-pudding of a novel stuffed with chivalrous, legendary nonsense and a crowd of eccentrics who keep telling each other stories. One of the tales about a gluttonous shepherd is excellent. He wrote many poems and short prose works, some excellent, some that are casual and scrappy.

Galt was a sea-captain's son. Educated at Greenock Academy, he worked as a Clyde port customs clerk; wrote essays, verses, tales for local journals; studied law in London; toured European ports as a merchant's agent seeking ways to break Napoleon's embargo on British goods; became secretary of a company settling immigrants in Canada where he also became a British government agent. He opened new roads and founded the city of Guelph in Ontario; returned to lobby parliament on behalf of Canadians who had been promised compensation for losses got by supporting Britain against the USA; failed after months of effort; would have died poor had he not written text books, travel books and novels, once writing himself out of debtors' jail.

Galt's novels let us see and enjoy the changing nature of life between 1760 when George III was crowned and 1832 when the Reform Bill was passed. He called them *treatises on the history of society*, though few treatises are as entertaining. Goldsmith's *Vicar of Wakefield* has an English country clergyman as narrator-hero; Galt decided to translate the same poor, kind, honest simple-minded family man into the Church of Scotland, but the result has a wholly different plot. Goldsmith's Dr Primrose is shown dealing with only two parishioners: a fashionable landowner who nearly destroys the vicar's family while trying to seduce his daughters, and a modest nobleman who helps the good people reach a happy ending. The setting is the static social world of nearly all fiction before Walter Scott's, a world with an almost uncrossable barrier between aristocrats and professional folk and where the few manual workers who appear are mainly servants, comic or villainous or both. Political events are heard as distant rumours, but usually, as in *The Vicar of Wakefield*, never mentioned.

Galt's Rev. Micah Balwhidder in *The Annals of the*

Parish describes the fifty years of his ministry from 1760 to 1810 in fifty short chapters, each a story in itself about his dealings with parishioners in every social class from lord to village idiot. The stories are funny or sad; contain love affairs, a murder, financial losses and gains; we gradually see the parish is being changed faster and faster by forces from outside. It lies between the Clyde ports and Glasgow so benefits from both legal trade and smuggling. In 1761 smuggling cheapens the cost of tea and common people start drinking it, even poor old women who till then had only drunk home-brewed ale. Balwhidder gently, firmly breaks up a tea-party because he opposes smuggling and because such parties encourage gossip. In the following year an impoverished gentlewoman starts selling tea openly. He starts buying it to assist her, and is surprised to discover *that it did no harm to the heads of the drinkers, which was not always the case with the possets that were in fashion before*. Balwhidder (twice widowed, thrice married) has for a second wife a farmer's daughter with *a geni for management*. She starts a dairy and upsets him by making *the manse merely to be a factory of butter and cheese, and to breed up veal calves for the slaughter*. She works late into the night spinning and carding thread, leaving him lonely in the parlour. This makes him too sad to read or write so she removes the candles because now he obviously does not need them. In 1788 a rich incomer builds a large cotton mill and employs weavers who double the parish population. That and the opening of coal mines makes some folk richer but also (Balwhidder thinks) more selfish. He preaches sermons urging charity toward the needy and is astonished when former friends shun him as *a black-neb* – a Radical who favours Revolution. Improved roads, a stage-coach service and bookshop lead working folk to reading and discussing the atheist and utilitarian ideas of Paine, Mill and Bentham who say society should be founded on fraternity, social equality, philanthropy and universal benevolence. Balwhidder preaches that these are simply new-fangled names for Christian love and charity, so the weavers leave his church and found their own meeting house. He can remember 1776 when a cottager shocked the whole parish by leaving his wife and enlisting to fight the American rebels: but now nobody seems surprised when twenty or thirty local men enlist to fight the French.

Here is a short specimen of Micah Balwhidder's prose.

I have now to note a curious thing, not on account of its importance, but to show to what lengths a correspondence had been opened in the parish with the furthest parts of the earth. Mr Cayenne got a turtle-fish sent to him from a Glasgow merchant, and it was living when it came to the Wheatrig House, and was one of the most remarkable beasts that had ever been seen in our country side. It weighed as much as a well-fed calf, and had three kinds of meat in its body, fish, flesh, and fowl, and it had four water-wings, for they could not properly be called fins; but what was little short of a miracle about the creature, happened after the head was cutted off, when, if a finger was offered to it, it would open its mouth and snap at it, and all this after the carcass was divided for dressing.

Apart from *cutted* instead of cut, all these words are common to England and Scotland, yet how Scottish it sounds! The turtle is being described by a man with a lively interest in what he sees and a wish to convey it. This was common among travellers and seamen in 17th-century England, and perhaps for that reason seemed naïve and ill-bred a century later, when such descriptions could be left to those making a science of zoo-ology. But this is Balwhidder's prose, not Galt's, and the voices in his other books, though as precise, have a more rural or mercantile or legal ring according to character.

Galt's *The Provost* is a similar chronicle of country-town life by a thrice-chosen chief magistrate; *The Member* gives the life of a Scots MP elected three times by English rotten boroughs. The first is also a linen-draper who ensures that every civic improvement, disaster, festival and government subsidy enriches him; the second a nabob – a merchant enriched by trade with India, who switches to manipulating House of Commons backstairs business in order to give jobs to his needy relations. Before the 1970s most British people thought such types were extinct in local and central government. If so, we now know they have returned in force.

To Galt's best books add Hogg's tales of farming life, Scott's *Antiquary*, *The Two Drovers*, *The Highland Widow* and nearly all Burns's poetry. The result is a uniquely whole view of a small but complex nation over several decades around 1800. Galt's politics were liberal, Scott's were Tory, certainly Burns's and probably Hogg's were radical, but the four shared a democratic vision. Perhaps only Burns and Hogg believed everyone should have a vote in their government, but all believed rulers should listen to what folk in every social class had to say: tramps, idiots and criminals included. They were stimulated by the thought that Scotland was travelling from a wildly legendary past into a future enriched by new trade, science and industry. But the new forces would soon make folk with their breadth of social knowledge and sympathy as impossible in Scotland as it had long been in England.

Notes

Scott's novels are available in many different editions.

Canongate Classic no. 87, *The Journal of Sir Walter Scott*, edited and introduced by W.E.K. Anderson, 1998.

Canongate Classic no. 39, James Hogg, *Confessions of a Justified Sinner*, edited and introduced by David Groves, 1996, '99.

Selected Stories and Sketches by James Hogg, edited by Douglas Mack, Scottish Academic Press.

Canongate Classic no.74, James Hogg, *The Three Perils of Man*, edited and introduced by Douglas Gifford, 1989, '96.

Canongate Classic no. 71, John Galt, *The Member* and *The Radical*, introduced by Paul H. Scott, 1996.

CHAPTER EIGHT

Nineteenth-century Emigrants

THE GREAT BRITISH poets born towards the end of the 18th century disagreed about many things but believed what Tom Paine argued in *The Rights of Man*: that the poorest people have as much right to choose their government as the richest, and democracy will make Britain better for all. So from 1780 onward groups of employers and manual workers campaigned, sometimes together, for the right to vote.

By 1832 all the great radical poets were dead except Wordsworth and Coleridge, who had lost faith in democracy. The parliamentary Reform Bill of that year only gave the vote to Britons who could afford to keep a good home and servants, since landlords, professional folk and factory owners agreed that votes for manual workers would give them the means of raising their wages. That would damage the nation by reducing company profits and breaking the laws of political economy as revised by

Malthus. He was an English clergyman who proved arithmetically that a population will always grow too large for the food it needs if families of the poor are not constantly culled by hunger and disease; so schemes of public welfare must always lead to public disaster. The reformed parliament agreed. Thanks to steam-powered inventions, the defeat of Napoleon and the strongest existing navy, Britain now had the biggest and most profitable empire on earth with the wealthiest aristocracy and middle classes. Meanwhile her labourers' lives in field and factory grew increasingly squalid. Her subjects had liberty to make as much money as they legally could, but social equality and trade union fraternity were banned.

To control *the masses* (as they were now called) representatives of the prosperous *classes* had made Australia a jail for thieves and poachers and trade unionists, put military barracks beside every fast-growing factory town, organised a modern police force. For destitute orphans and the infirm the unemployed workhouses were created: *places pleasantly so-called,* said Thomas Carlyle, *because no work can be done in them.* It was he who told the British that they had entered *the mechanical age. Nothing is now done directly, or by hand; all is by rule and calculated contrivance . . . The shuttle drops from the fingers of the weaver, and falls into iron fingers that ply it faster.* Hence periodic unemployment *and the shoemaker's child running barefoot, as her father has made too many shoes.*

A Calvinist stonemason's son, Carlyle had mastered languages at Edinburgh University, become a school teacher and then (through marriage) a farmer in Dumfriesshire while writing articles for the *Encyclopaedia Britannica*, translating German literature and corresponding with Goethe. He had lost faith in biblical Christianity but never denounced it because he admired all faiths that could inspire actions; and would have liked one himself. He had no faith in political economists who viewed Britain as a statistical machine profiting those who ran it by grinding those who did not into oblivion. British churchmen said the laws of this machine were the laws of God; atheists that they were the laws of nature. Viewed from the standpoint of the labouring class into which Carlyle had been born they were a nightmare hard to awaken from. Reading German freed Carlyle from it. Germany with her forty universities was still a cluster of rural kingdoms and city states loosely connected by language and a growing literature. She had no factory system yet, and was existing as an idea while waiting to become a nation, so her poets and philosophers thought societies were shaped by ideas, not economic laws – ideas like Christianity, Chivalry, Democracy, etc. In Goethe's *Faust* the world is described as a garment woven by nature to make god visible to us. Carlyle believed god, truth and justice were the same, so no unjust system could last. To prove it he wrote his history of *The French Revolution*, a work that needed the resources of the British Museum library. He and his wife sold the farm and flitted to London.

The history was written to warn and challenge smug governments and people everywhere, but especially in Britain. It is written completely in the present tense and shows history being shaped by feelings, not statistics. A multitude of people appear in vivid action like a speeded-up film, some close-up, many at a distance. A grimly ironic humour runs through the work like the humour of *Sir Patrick Spens*, that says the Scots lords on a sinking ship hated wetting their shoes but the water was soon over their hats. Yet Carlyle is not pitiless. He regrets the deaths of poor brave Marie Antoinette and her muddle-headed husband, but says history would be meaningless if the French had NOT risen against the extravagant, incompetent, long-established rulers who had steered their nation, the most fertile European land, into total bankruptcy. He says that a hungry mob of Parisian mothers storming the Palace of Versailles did better than nearly a million Irish peasants starving to death in a place blessed by English landlords and British economists; says the death and disappearance of the infant French crown prince is as lamentable as (not worse than) the deaths of many British orphans through brutal labour in weaving sheds and coal mines; says that the average number of aristocrats and revolutionary leaders beheaded each day at the height of the Reign of Terror was not greater than the number of Britons, mostly destitute, some of them twelve-year-old children, hanged for petty theft over the same period. He says most wailings over the fate of a graceful aristocracy come from feeling that a social class who kept themselves above social distresses for over a century should NEVER suffer like the common people under them.

The prose of Carlyle's book starts calmly but works itself into rhythms that match moods of things described, rising to such sentences as *Insurrectionary chaos surrounds the palace like ocean around diving bell.* Like Douglas in his *Aeneis*, Spenser in *The Faery Queen*, Milton in *Paradise Lost*, Carlyle invented a special language for his epic. It mixes all the rhetorical devices known to Scots preachers with a semi-Germanic grammar and a vocabulary of biblical, technical and slang terms, beside invented words of his own. He described it as *a Babylonish dialect*, quoting what Dr Johnson said about Milton's language. Like the bible, *Paradise Lost*, Joyce's *Ulysses* and even (I suspect) Tolstoy's *War and Peace*, the depth and breadth of this book will weary readers who try to swallow it fast. But it is worth absorbing.

Carlyle was a democrat when he wrote it, for which reason European monarchies had it banned. Later, alas, he despaired of democracy, advocated slavery and dictatorship, but never ceased to doubt the glories of Victorian civilization, so was widely regarded as Britain's national conscience.

Edward Irvine, a friend of Carlyle, was a popular Church of Scotland minister who preceded him to London. His sermons had especially inspired women in Clydeside congregations and one of these, a seaman's wife, also came to London, supporting her family by needlework after her husband was paralysed in a shipping accident. Before dying, probably of overwork (sewing was notoriously ill-paid), she managed to place her eight-year-old son, James Thomson, in a Church of Scotland London orphanage. Education there let him become an army schoolmaster in Ireland when the army was helping landlords evict their least profitable tenants. Sacked for insubordination (he may have been drunk) Thomson mostly lived a bed-sitting room life by various ill-paid clerking jobs and freelance journalism. He learned the art of poetry while translating Heine and Leopardi. In 1874 his greatest work *The City of Dreadful Night* was serialised in a rationalist journal, *The National Reformer*, under the pen-name Bysshe Vanolis. Bysshe was Shelley's second name, Vanolis a distortion of Novalis, a German poet whose work Thomson also loved. Like most other late 19th-century Scots writers (several of whom came south to live by journalism) Thomson worked in an English context that needs more explanation.

All the great radical poets of earlier years were labelled 'Romantic' by Victorians who loved their verses but not their ideas. So Burns was enjoyed as an excuse for jolly banquets, Blake as an unworldly eccentric, Wordsworth as a guide to natural scenery, Coleridge as a guide to exotic scenery, Byron as a fascinating cynic, Shelley as a beautiful but ineffectual angel, and Keats as the most Romantic of all. Keats's last three great odes were written as he died of consumption when twenty-six. In lovely musical speech they compare the lasting beauty of art with the disappointments of life, and they avoid 18th-century diction by using a slightly Elizabethan diction. Victorians enriched by industrialism but unhappy about working-class poverty and pollution felt such melancholy beauty was as high as English poetry could reach. Burns, Shelley and Byron had condemned the state of Britain with a high-spirited confidence in human vitality. Tennyson, Matthew Arnold and Thomas Hardy lamented the state of Britain in low-spirited verse regretting the absence of a God who would rule things better. The poet whose will and brain were strongest, Gerald Manley Hopkins, gained faith in God AND humanity by working as a priest for the poorest folk in Wales, England and Scotland. Yet these writers had been born into or had entered the affluent classes! Bysshe Vanolis had not. Journals that bought his writings ceased publication. Despite words of encouragement from George Eliot, Rossetti and Meredith he died destitute from cancer of the bowels in a London charity hospital.

The City of Dreadful Night starts thus:

Lo, thus, as prostrate, 'In the dust I write
  My heart's deep languor and my soul's sad
    tears.'
Yet why evoke the spectres of black night
  To blot the sunshine of exultant years?

Why disinter dead faith from mouldering
  hidden?
Why break the seals of mute despair unbidden,
  And wail life's discords into careless ears?

Because a cold rage seizes one at whiles
  To show the bitter old and wrinkled truth
Stripped naked of all vesture that beguiles,
  False dreams, false hopes, false masks and
    modes of youth;
Because it gives some sense of power and
  passion
In helpless impotence to try to fashion
  Our woe in living words howe'er uncouth.

Surely I write not for the hopeful young,
  Or those who deem their happiness of worth,
Or such as pasture and grow fat among
  The shows of life and feel nor doubt nor
    dearth,
Or pious spirits with a God above them
To sanctify and glorify and love them,
  Or sages who foresee a heaven on earth.

Poshly flowing, semi-archaic terms like *heart's deep languor* and *vesture that beguiles* are typical late-Victorian poetic diction, but a more colourful, more pungent, more colloquial speech would not fit the modern hell Thomson describes. Dante, Milton and Shelley's hells are crowded cities full of talk and social turmoil. Thomson's is a modern city where the sun never rises and sleepless people wander dark streets without love, faith or hope. They are kept from suicide by memories of these. Their god is endurance who, like Dürer's *Melancholia*, broods on a mountain above the city with her feet among unemployed tools of trade and science. This hell is known to all who have been homeless or afraid to go home.

Shakespeare described a meaningless universe long before Thomson and in more memorable words, but his usual mouthpieces are half-crazed kings – important folk. Even Parolles – the exposed cheat and coward who says *Simply the things I am shall make me live* – has a name and character. The people of the city are anonymous and, apart from a cripple trying to revert to infancy, all grimly stoical. Macbeth and Lear have earned their hell by wrong actions. In Thomson's hell nobody has been notably wicked. Some remember an existence in which they tried to fight injustice or do good things, but having wakened *to this real night* they know they are remembering an illusion. This hell is not dull to read about because negation is enacted through a surprising wealth of images. In one episode the poet shelters in the porch of a deserted church. It contains a sculpture of a sphinx menacing an angel holding an upright sword. Dozing, the poet is wakened by a crash. The angel's wings have fallen off. Dozing again, another sharp noise rouses him. The sword has broken off, the sphinx now menaces an unarmed man. Again the doze, the crash. The man's head has fallen off and rolled between the sphinx's paws. If, like ancient Egyptians and Grecians, we see the sphinx as universal nature with her nurturing madonna's breast and devouring lion's rear, then her opponent is three historic periods. As angel he is Christian mankind, appearing greater than nature through faith in God. Wingless but sword in hand he becomes 18th-century man whose reasoning powers make him nature's equal, if not superior. Swordless he is post-Darwinian man, as temporary as other creatures nature has born and more likely to lose his head.

If *The City of Dreadful Night* is placed between Shelley's *Peter Bell* and Eliot's *Waste Land* it becomes part of an English tradition of cities gone wrong. Beside work by Leopardi, Schopenhauer, Baudelaire, Thomas Hardy, Herman Melville and the later Mark Twain it counterblasts a 19th-century belief in everlasting human progress. To those who know terrible depressions it may give courage, as Thomson intended, by saying *You are not alone – endure!* But what if we ask Hamlet's question *Why?* Why should we endure painful lives?

John Davidson, ex-schoolteacher struggling to live in London by all kinds of writing, thought Nietzsche told why: Nietzsche who said all religious, philosophic or political systems that explain life comfortably are delusions; life can only be justified by those with the strength to enjoy as well as endure it at its worst. This extract from Thomson's *Testament of a Man Forbid* tries to show how.

This Beauty, this Divinity, this Thought,
This hallowed bower and harvest of delight
Whose roots ethereal seemed to clutch the stars,
Whose amaranths perfumed eternity,
Is fixed in earthly soil enriched with bones
Of used-up workers; fattened with the blood
Of prostitutes, the prime manure; and dressed
With brains of madmen and the broken hearts
Of children. Understand it, you at least
Who toil all day and writhe and groan all night
With roots of luxury, a cancer struck
In every muscle; out of you it is
Cathedrals rise and Heaven blossoms fair;
You are the hidden putrefying source

> Of beauty and delight, of leisured hours,
> Of passionate loves and high imaginings;
> You are the dung that keeps the roses sweet.

The defect in these lines is the high-falutin Romantic phrases, the *hallowed bower* and *roots ethereal* that separate the speaker from folk he's supposed to be addressing. It is easy to imagine a well-educated landlord or stockbroker telling the poet, 'yes, things have to be like that, but there's no point in talking about it. You'll only upset people.'

Davidson's best poem, *Thirty Bob a Week*, is the monologue of a cockney office clerk supporting a family on the lowest possible wage. He knows he is one of millions but refuses to see himself as a victim of chance. He feels a power in himself which would squash others flat if allowed scope, so the power of his boss strikes him as natural, to be accepted with a sardonic shrug. The poem is profounder than my glib summary suggests. By giving the personal and universal without sweetly blending them – the World as Will in the soul of a harried commuter – Davidson presents the secular religion of most folk today, and does it by abandoning the clichés of Victorian adventure fiction that a badly paid clerk then would find handiest when dramatising his place in the world:

It's a naked child against a hungry wolf;
 It's playing bowls upon a splitting wreck;
It's walking on a string across a gulf
 With millstones fore-and-aft about your neck;
But the thing is daily done by many and many a
 one;
 And we fall, face forward, fighting, on the deck.

Believing he had failed as a poet Davidson drowned himself in 1909. But T.S. Eliot said the clerk in *Thirty Bob a Week* haunted him all his life. Hugh MacDiarmid was seventeen when he read a newspaper report of Davidson's body being found on an English Channel beach. Later he said he imagined it *like a bullet-hole in a landscape: God seen through the wrong end of a telescope.*

Before considering MacDiarmid we should look at a writer who gave and still gives readers more pleasure than Carlyle, Thomson, Davidson and MacDiarmid added together. Like Poe and Oscar Wilde he has a far bigger reputation overseas than in his native land.

Robert Louis Stevenson (1850–95) came from three generations of lighthouse-building engineers and grew up in Edinburgh. His imagination was strongly fired by Scots legend and folk history, first through a Calvinist nursemaid (*My second mother, my first wife, the angel of my infant life*), followed by the writings of Burns and Scott. Poor health stopped him entering the family business and from young manhood on forced him to live in warmer lands. A strong story-telling imagination and need to justify himself by hard work made him a professional writer and at last a rich one. Before then, while subsidised by a stern but loving dad whose religion he rejected after reading Darwin, he met an American woman ten years his senior with a son by a failing marriage. When she returned to California he pursued her there, travelling as the poorest sort of emigrant and weakening his lungs. They married, and her nursing prolonged his life while he sought good health, sometimes enjoying spells of it, in the USA, Switzerland, south England and finally Samoa. Like Scott at Abbotsford he died famous on an estate bought with the earnings of his pen. His poems, essays, travel writings, reminiscences, short stories, novellas and novels were published in twenty-four volumes after his death and are mostly still in print.

Stevenson, like Scott, wished to write pleasant entertainments with happy endings, but as true to life as possible. He therefore divided writing into dramas and romances: dramas are plays that can be tragic, romances are novels that need not be. He explains this in his essay, *A Gossip about Romance*, which says life is mostly a response to events we have not chosen, and that:

> the interest turns, not upon what a man shall choose to do, but on how he manages to do it; not on the passionate slips and hesitations of the conscience, but on the problems of the body and of the practical intelligence, in clean, open air adventure, the shock of arms and the diplomacy of life. With such materials as this it is impossible to build a play, for the serious theatre exists solely on moral grounds, and is a standing proof of the dissemination of the human conscience. But it is possible to build, upon this ground, the most joyous of verses, and the most lively, beautiful, and buoyant tales.

Treasure Island and *Kidnapped* are masterpieces of that sort of tale. Both describe poor boys who seek fortunes and, after convincingly fearful adventures that hide a fairy tale twist, become rich young gents. But most of the other tales are well-written shockers driven by devices common to both Victorian popular novels and plays: body-snatching, ship-wrecking, secret societies, anarchists, sinister mormons, wicked Renaissance nobles, a fascinating vampire. None of these tales are very buoyant. The most wonderfully told is the tale of the middle-class bachelor who can only enjoy sex with prostitutes when changed by a debasing drug: a mainly true-to-life tale, though sexually insecure men usually debase their characters with alcohol.

After *Treasure Island*, *Kidnapped*, *Dr Jekyll and Mr Hyde*, Stevenson's best work is *The Master of Ballantrae*, a novel in which an honest, conscientious, hard-working man is exploited, maddened and corrupted by his devilishly attractive, mean-spirited brother. It is a tragedy. Even better writing, more interesting people and scenery are in *Weir of Hermiston* which Stevenson did not live to finish, and which also tended toward tragedy. Except in the short, widely ignored novella *John Nicholson* Stevenson set all his good imaginative work about Scotland in the 18th century, none in his own. Why?

Partly because of exile enforced by poor health, mainly because Scotland had become a province – a land whose rulers and writers chiefly saw it from the standpoint of a distant capital city, so could not see clearly. The Glasgow conurbation had become the second largest city in Britain when London was the biggest city in the world, partly because most British battleships were being built on Clydeside. Its slums were the worst in Europe, its municipal water supply, public transport system and electric lighting the most modern, yet James Barrie was foremost among a set of popular writers (sometimes called 'The Kailyard' or 'Cabbage Patch' school) who depicted a Scotland of quaint, loveable, noble or weird rustics. The highlands were the most fictionally falsified. Having been most savagely exploited by increasingly absentee landlords, and having put up a resistance that sent a small new political party to Westminster, their glens and islands were represented as provinces of fairyland. Stevenson had nothing to do with such falsities.

How Scotland provincialised herself, then began to win free of that state, belongs to the next chapter.

Notes

Selected Writings by Thomas Carlyle, edited with an introduction by Alan Shelston, Penguin Books, 1971.

The French Revolution by Thomas Carlyle. London, 1900 Library of English Classics.

Canongate Classics no. 53, *The City of Dreadful Night* by James Thomson introduced by Edwin Morgan, 1993.

Places of the Mind, a biography of James Thomson by Tom Leonard, Jonathan Cape, London, 1993.

The Poems of John Davidson, edited by Andrew Trumball, 2 vols, Edinburgh and London, 1973.

Canongate Classics no. 58, *The Scottish Novels* by Robert Louis Stevenson (*Kidnapped/Catriona/ The Master of Ballantrae, Weir of Hermiston*), introduced by Jenni Calder and Roderick Watson, 1995.

Canongate Classics no. 61, *Markheim, Jekyll and the Merry Men: Shorter Scottish Fiction* by Robert Louis Stevenson, introduced by Roderick Watson, 1995.

Canongate Classics no. 72, *Tales of the South Seas* by Robert Louis Stevenson, introduced by Jenni Calder, 1996.

Canongate Classics no. 77, *Tales of Adventure* by Robert Louis Stevenson, edited and introduced by Francis Hart, 1997.

CHAPTER NINE

The Twentieth Century, Mainly

SCOTLAND HAD THE most literate working class in Britain, so throughout the 19th century a higher proportion of Scots went to well-paid jobs in an expanding commercial empire. This empire needed such a multitude of literate employees that in 1875 a British government made the Scottish local school system compulsory in England too, but before that Scots schools and universities had become centres of Anglicisation. Their best pupils were competing for jobs under English legislations on every continent but Antarctica; Scots history and classics helped nobody pass English civil service exams, so teachers and lecturers ignored them and punished highland and lowland children for talking the language of their parents. Galt had said Scots writers were lucky to have a native Scots vocabulary on top of an English one. By 1900 that extra resource was an official disadvantage. By 1900 also the *Encyclopaedia Britannica*, whose prestige and scholarship had steadily expanded, was passing into USA ownership through the immediate agency of the *London Times*. To conform easily with foreign bosses, many Scots began advertising themselves as competent unemotional men who spoke seldom and spoke to the point. This national stereotype has been around for two and a half millennia because it can given even fools an aspect of sphinx-like omniscience. When they acquired an empire Spartans, Romans, Spanish Hidalgos and English aristocrats adopted it. To make a Scottish version acceptable outside their native land Scots mediocrities emphasised their quaintly selfish caution. *Remember a Scotsman's proudest characteristic, Maggie*, a Scots MP in Barrie's play *What Every Woman Knows* tells his wife, *he will never do anything to damage his career.* English audiences laughed appreciatively.

Yet despite its provincial state, its smug middle class, its steady outflow of emigrants seeking better lives elsewhere, 20th-century Scotland again got writers who imagined life here without quaintness or nostalgia and dispensed with that curse of British fiction, the honest hero who comes to a happy middle-class end.

The House with the Green Shutters was published in 1901 and counterblasted the Kailyard school of fiction by showing a lowland country town where people are selfish, cunning and spiteful. They are dominated by Gourlay on whose carting business all their trade depends, and are both agents and chorus in his tragedy. It is a book fit to stand beside *Wuthering Heights* and *The Mayor of Casterbridge*, though sexual love has no part in it. The author, George Douglas Brown, was the bastard child of an Ayrshire farmer and his Irish servant. At Glasgow University he studied great Greek dramas about King's families destroying themselves, won a scholarship to Oxford, but obtained a poor degree there because study was interrupted by a spell at home nursing his dying mother. He then lived by small literary jobs in the Home Counties, wrote his single masterpiece, and died of an undiagnosed illness a year after publication.

The book has four main characters.

1 Gourlay, whose great energy is all in pride of power and possessions. He is full of courage but can only sympathise with completely obedient underlings who depend on him, so is a selfish brute.

2 His son, whose energy runs all to imagination and who (according to a schoolteacher), has a *sensory perceptiveness in gross excess of his intellectuality*, so is a selfish coward.

3 Gourlay's wife, a sick woman who has nothing but

feeble indulging sympathy for her son and lonely stoicism for herself.

These three are fools because intelligence is a union of courage, imagination and sympathy, but are not contemptible fools because each (especially father and son) are lively embodiments of parts essential to a good human being, though destructive when isolated. The fourth character is Wilson, the provision merchant whose superior cunning and modern business methods let him replace Gourlay as the town's great man and finally ruin him. The tragedy is enjoyable through the dramatic clarity and black comedy of plot and language. It has one fault: the provincialism of sometimes pausing to tell the reader how *Scottish* the story is instead of leaving that to the events.

That fault almost wrecks *Gillespie*, with the worst first chapter that ever introduced a novel worth reading. The author, John MacDougall Hay, was from the Gaelic fishing village of Tarbert in Argyll. He became a highland schoolmaster, then a Church of Scotland minister near Glasgow, and his novel describes an interestingly repulsive small-town capitalist of a sort who was reshaping the world as well as Scotland. But Hay at first has so little confidence in his subject that Gillespie is described being born in horridly weird and improbable Scottish circumstances, and in the prose of cheap romantic fiction. *She was a Macmillan, lissom, white as milk, red as the dawn.* How can such words lead to an interesting, believable tale? Yet they do.

Gillespie starts as a grocer (like Gourlay's rival) but in a coastal town with a fishing fleet and farms on a hillside behind. We see this sly, mean, humourless man use new methods of communication and transport, use the local banker and lawyer, use the accidents of good weather and bad, use the greed and needs of others till he at last owns farms and the fishing fleet. He is praised as his community's saviour then hated as its exploiter, and his success does come to seem supernatural, not because he has given his soul to Satan but because he seems to have none. Profit is his only motive, he feels for nothing else. Thus, when shut in the dark with a recently drowned headless body that starts jerking about, his companions go mad with fear but he stays calm, realising the corpse must have a large eel inside. He is not even malicious. By a piece of sharp legal practice he double-crosses a colleague out of property. When the victim strikes his face he smiles and advises the assailant not to do it again – there is a witness present and another blow will make the attacker liable to pay Gillespie even more money by legal process. *Ye damned jelly fish!* roars his victim.

Gillespie is half told from the standpoint of a woman whose home he destroys. Like the works of Walter Scott it is good, but not throughout. He wrote another novel, *Barnacles*, which is very bad throughout.

The trouble was that Scotland lacked journals and critics who would open public debate about good new work. In the USA Hawthorne's tales had been welcomingly reviewed by Poe and Herman Melville. The early works of D.H. Lawrence, James Joyce, T.S. Eliot were publicised by Ford Madox Ford and Ezra Pound. Scotland's best reviewer, Catherine Carswell, was sacked by the *Glasgow Herald* for praising D.H. Lawrence's *Women in Love*. And the best Scottish poet since Robert Burns only received encouraging reviews of his early poetry because he wrote the poetry under a pen-name, Hugh MacDiarmid, and the reviews under his baptismal name, Christopher Grieve. This was how he overcame the provincialism of the Scottish press.

MacDiarmid's dad was a postman in the mill town of Langholm, five miles north of the English border. His mother was caretaker of the town library and the family lived beneath it, so the boy had free access. His appetite for poetry, biography, travel, Darwinian science, dictionaries and histories of ideas grew by what it fed on; he discarded his parents' Evangelical Christianity and decided to be a poet. His taste for encyclopaedic surveys would have prevented this without a philosophy and faith to order it. He found both in the poetry of John Davidson who, when poetry was widely supposed to be sired on Fine Feelings by Classical Education, believed that poets need strong stomachs to see how most folk live, strong heads to see the universe opened by modern science, and that the only good which makes sense of life is mental fight, not a metaphysical provision. This was the faith of Blake, Tom Paine, Shelley, Shaw and (with less hope of a happy outcome) Thomas Hardy. It may have been the faith of Jesus when he told his followers to take up their cross and follow him. The people most likely to scorn it nowadays are not Christians but people who need no faith because they feel the world is, for the most part, sufficiently comfortable. MacDiarmid brought to this fight the buoyancy of Walt Whitman and often quoted his lines, *Do I contradict myself? Very well, then, I contradict myself; I am vast – I contain multitudes.*

After working as a journalist for several small newspapers MacDiarmid had a fairly easy '14–'18 War as medical orderly in Thessalonica; then returned to Scotland determined to shake life into this zombie of a nation where scientific discovery and invention were still possible but social life was mainly ruled by schoolteachers and Church of Scotland clergy, while most poetry was pastiche Burns minus satire and politics. MacDiarmid's first instruments were three literary magazines he founded and edited from a council house in Montrose, the east coast town where he supported himself by reporting for the local newspaper. His magazines attacked most of what was then admired in modern Scottish art and literature and praised the rarer items he found good. In these he published his first poems using a new sort of lowland Scots: the border dialect he had been taught NOT to use at school, but enlarged with words from many other Scots districts and from writings by the earliest makers, Henryson, Dunbar and Douglas. From *Jamieson's Etymological Dictionary of the Scottish Language* he took words that had been obsolete for centuries but evoked states of mind he could not reach through well-known English words. Critics denounced this unusually broad Scots as artificial, thus echoing Ben Jonson on Spenser's verse (*Spenser writ no language*) and Dr Johnson on Milton's (*a Babylonish dialect*). When I first read MacDiarmid's lyrics in my late teens I thought they entertained the ear more than the brain but kept remembering them until their intelligence dawned on me. I was the more convinced of their goodness because convinced against my will.

THE BONNIE BROUKIT BAIRN

Mars is braw in crammasy, — crimson velvet
Venus in a green silk goun,
The auld mune shak's her gowden feathers,
Their starry talk's a wheen — abundance
  o' blethers, — empty speech
Nane for thee a thochtie sparin',
Earth, thou bonnie broukit — broken/hurt/neglected
  bairn!
—But greet, an' in your tears ye'll droun — weep
The haill clanjamfrie! — whole rabble

A modern poem making a big statement about the universe must take account of earlier views. Long before Galileo's telescope showed sun spots and lunar craters the ancient pagans had called our stars and planets gods; Jews and Christians called them creations of one great God, but all agreed that earth was the only part of the universe where alteration, pain and death occurred. Heavenly bodies were perfect and eternal. A harmony inaudible to earthly ears was supposed to keep heavenly bodies moving in regular paths without colliding. After admitting the beauty of Mars and Venus this poem describes the moon (goddess of chastity) as an old spinster flaunting her wealth, and calls the music of the spheres *blethers* because these heavenly beings ignore the dirty little earth. The tone is that of a Scots Calvinist condemning Catholic ritual or a Communist denouncing aristocracy, yet the tenderness of the sixth line introduces a modern astronomical idea: the earth is a tiny body on the periphery of the universe, not (as pagans, Jews and Christians had thought) its diseased but essential hub. The poet is therefore siding with the earth against a modern idea he believes, as well as an ancient one he rejects. But his working-class prejudice for our planet is not a reason for demeaning others. The poem would be trivial rhetoric without the last two lines.

> —But greet, an' in your tears ye'll droun
> The haill clanjamfrie.

The stars grow dim and are extinguished when seen through eyes in which tears gather. The only life and mind in our solar system is on this planet, and we have no proof of it existing elsewhere in the universe, and nobody now believes the infinity of stars we can see at night are intelligences. Only such minds as ours can lend them awareness, so there is some reason in preferring human grief to the multitude of the heavenly host. Christianity believes that in zero AD God preferred that too.

Like most westerners MacDiarmid was haunted by the God Christianity had adopted from the Jews, but never quite trusted Him.

THE WATERGAW

Ae weet forenicht i' the yow-trummle
I saw yon antrin thing,
A watergaw wi' its chitterin' licht
Ayont the on-ding;
An' I thocht o' the last wild look ye gied
Afore ye deed!

There was nae reek i' the laverock's hoose
That nicht – an' nane i' mine;
But I hae thocht o' that foolish licht
Ever sin' syne;
An' I think that mebbe at last I ken
What your look meant then.

Prose translation. One wet fortnight in the cold sheep-shearing month I saw that queer thing, a fragment of pale rainbow, its light trembling behind the misty rain beating on me, and I thought of the last wild look you gave before you died. The night then had no cloud in the skylark's house (meaning sky) and no haze of smoke in mine, but I have thought ever since of that foolish light, and think maybe at last I know what your look meant then.

In *Genesis* the full rainbow arch is God's promise that he will never again destroy life in a universal deluge. It became a sign of hope. The watergaw is therefore a sign of hope broken, trembling within a storm but not wholly quenched. The second verse recalls a night sky clear enough to suggest a soaring, tuneful lark by day. It has only clarity in common with the air of a death chamber, but the last wild look of the dying man (he was MacDiarmid's father) has something in common with the watergaw. The meaning of that look and this poem can be put in no further words without loss of meaning.

I have read appreciations of these two lyrics by critics who value them as much as I do yet explain them quite differently: a sure proof of their greatness. They appeared in *Sangschaw*, a book published in 1925. In December that year MacDiarmid had this advert for his greatest work printed in the *Glasgow Herald*.

> Mr Hugh MacDiarmid has now completed a gallimaufry in braid Scots verse, entitled 'A Drunk Man Looks at the Thistle'. It is in fact, a long poem of over a thousand lines split up into several sections, but the forms within the sections range from ballad measure to vers libre. The matter includes satire, amphigouri, lyrics, parodies of Mr T.S. Eliot and other poets, and translations from the Russian, French, and German. The whole poem is in braid Scots, except a few quatrains which are in the nature of a skit on Mr Eliot's 'Sweeney' poems, and it has been expressly designed to show that braid Scots can be effectively applied to all manner of subjects and measures.

He did not complete *A Drunk Man Looks at the Thistle* in 1925 but felt on the verge of completion because he was in the midst of it. And Eliot had supplied him with much more than material to satirise.

Joyce's *Ulysses* and Eliot's *The Waste Land* appeared in 1922 and MacDiarmid learned from both, for having written short lyrics embodying different states of mind, often contrary to each other, he wanted to make something larger and more epic. Joyce's interior monologues showed how one mind can flow through many states while conversing with itself in a variety of lingos, even when drunk or hallucinating or on the verge of sleep. Eliot's *Waste Land* describes a more metropolitan culture than MacDiarmid's complacently dull Scotland but one equally spoiled and misruled. Quotations, translations, pastiches of poets ancient and modern blend with Cockney pub gossip, ragtime popular songs and references to works of arctic exploration and anthropology. Commuters crowding over London Bridge are described in the words of Dante's vision of the damned in hell. Elizabethan blank verse describes the finely decorated room of a neurotic rich woman. A final hope of salvation is given in a commentary upon a Buddist scripture. Eliot had not yet declared his faith in Anglican religion and Conservative politics; his verse was ironic about the first and scathing about money-power. His working methods were an example to this Scot whose faith was in the Russian Revolution, whose scriptures were the works of Nietzsche, who took images for poetry, often with the words that conveyed them, from textbooks, biographies, prose fictions and foreign translation. As T.S. Eliot said, the inferior writer borrows, the good writer steals. That had been Shakespeare's practice also.

A Drunk Man Looks at the Thistle was 2,685 lines long when published in 1926. It is the blackly comic monologue of a poet, drunk in a ditch under the moon, staring at Scotland's national emblem. It and Scotland strike him as such grotesquely ugly, tough, common growths that the universe will be meaningless if he cannot manage to see some beauty in them. The poem's highest point is a metaphorical hymn to the 1926 General Strike with a lament for its failure. After many inventive high- and low-spirited twists and turns the poem ends in exhausted silence. The Scottish press condemned it for being coarsely vulgar, fashionably modernistic, stupidly archaic and far too political.

MacDiarmid was certainly political. In 1928 it became clear that the British Labour Party had dropped its early policy of independence for Scotland, so he became one of those who founded the Scottish National Party; it expelled him five years later because he thought small independent nations needed international communism to stop them growing parochial. He also thought international communism needed independent nations who preserved their character by resisting Moscow dictatorship, so the British communists expelled him. In *A Drunk Man Looks at the Thistle* he had said:

> I'll ha'e nae hauf-way hoose, but aye be whaur
> Extremes meet – it's the only way I ken

To dodge the curst conceit o' bein' richt
That damns the vast majority o' men.

And until 1929 his political campaigning, critical writing and poetry were funded by small-town newspaper reporting while he supported a wife and two children in a semi-detached council house. Then Compton Mackenzie invited him to edit a new magazine about British broadcasting. He and his family moved to London.

The magazine failed after three issues. His wife became mistress of a much older married man, a millionaire coal merchant. MacDiarmid entered a decade of living on loans and publishers' advances. In 1934 he and his new family moved as far from London as they could without falling into the North Atlantic: the island of Whalsay, in Shetland. In a cottage without gas or electricity, among fishermen neighbours whose rejected catch was a convenient article of diet, he wrote *On a Raised Beach*, one of his finest poems, using English diction and a deliberately hard geological vocabulary. Though internationally regarded as Scotland's greatest poet since Burns, accepted as that by Eliot, Walter de la Mare and Yeats, the Scots press mainly treated him as an embarrassing joke, the English press ignored him. During World War II, while left-wing English writers who had not fled to the USA were employed by the BBC or in government offices, MacDiarmid was directed into handling machine lathes in a Clydeside engineering works, then into keeping watch on a mine-sweeper. He wrote some pot-boiling books of an autobiographical sort but would have died in poverty had the Atlee government not given him a small civil-list pension.

Under these circumstances much of his later poetry is feeble – *chopped up prose*, as he said himself, yet even so, great lines often emerge. He described himself as a volcano throwing up some heat and flame among a great deal of smoke and ash. Like a volcano he was the product of terrible pressures, but he altered the cultural landscape of Scotland. Our universities have departments of Scottish Studies now, with courses in the older literature they ignored when MacDiarmid began writing. It also has a 20th-century literature which was poetically non-existent before he started making it. As Norman MacCaig said, *The bombs he threw erected buildings*, meaning that his belligerence against what he saw standing in the way of Scottish originality made it more possible.

The following poets were stimulated by MacDiarmid's example and often by his friendship: Goodsir Smith, Robert Garioch, Douglas Young and William Soutar who wrote their own variety of broad Scots, or Lallans as it was sometimes called; George Bruce and Hamish Henderson, who occasionally used it; Norman MacCaig who never used it; Somhairle MacGill-Eain (English, Sorley MacLean) who wrote in Gaelic. *The Golden Treasury of Scottish Poetry*, edited by MacDiarmid and published in 1940, was the first anthology to show Gaelic and Latin verses as essential parts of Scots literature, and MacGill-Eain helped the editor translate the Gaelic. Nearly all these poets lived and worked till near the end of the 20th century. In 2001 Bruce and Henderson are still with us. All eight deserve attention this book has no room to give, but room must be found for MacDiarmid's colleague in prose.

James Leslie Mitchell was born in 1901 at his parents' small upland farm in Aberdeenshire. From 1917–19 he was a journalist in Dundee, and then Glasgow, but was sacked for claiming cash for expenses then donating it to the Communist party. (He had joined on hearing of the Russian Revolution.) From 1919–23, he served the British army in Persia, India and Egypt, and from 1923–9, he was a clerk in the Royal Air Force and he wrote his first novel. From then on he supported a family by writing five non-fiction books (one about the state of Scotland in collaboration with MacDiarmid) and nine novels. He died in 1935 of overwork and a perforated ulcer. The three books most widely read and worth reading are *Sunset Song, Cloud Howe, Grey Granite*, a trilogy he marked off from the rest by writing them under the pen name, Lewis Grassic Gibbon. They are usually issued in one volume, *A Scots Quair*. Unlike his other novels they describe Scotland within his own lifespan (1901–35) with the local and historical grasp Scott brought to the place in 1745, or Galt around 1800.

The trilogy is seen mainly through the eyes of Chris Guthrie, whose childhood and young womanhood pass on a poor upland farm in Aberdeenshire until 1919, when the last of the Scots peasantry have died in World War I or had their way of life completely altered by it. As a young mother she moves to a nearby market town where a weaving mill employs most of the poorer families until the 1926 General Strike. Finally, as the mother of a young factory worker, she lives in an east coast industrial city where factories are recovering from the early 1930s depression through rearmament for the next world war. The most active characters in this pageant are men whom she supports with a kind of pitying wonder: a grim father brutalised by his struggle to win a living out of his poor farm; a first husband, also a farmer, kindly at first but brutalised by service in the 1914–18 war; her second husband, a Socialist minister who despairs of Christianity when the Labour Party sides with the Tories against trade unions and the unemployed; her son, a union organiser who rejects affection and propagates lies to serve the Communist party, the only organisation (he thinks) that truly aims to abolish poverty. Chris the daughter, wife and mother says very little yet is clearly stronger, wiser, more honest and affectionate than these men, but could not respect them, if they accepted society as it is. She has no idea how to improve it.

The narrative voice of the novel has enough east coast words to show it is working class, and their context usually makes them easy to understand. When not explaining things from the main character's viewpoint it speaks like the unidentified local gossips who call anybody richer or poorer than themselves *dirt* or *filth*, along with anything else honest or generous. Here they describe a local joiner.

> You couldn't get near his shop for the clutter of carts, half-made and half-broken, lying about, and the half of a churn, a hen-coop or so and God knows what – all left outside in the rain and sun while Ogilvie sat on a bench inside and wrote his ill bits of poetry and

> stite – he thought himself maybe a second Robert Burns. He was broad and big, a fell buirdly childe, and it seemed fell queer that a man like that couldn't settle down to the making of money, and him the last joiner in the place. But he'd tell you instead some rhyme or another, coarse dirt that was vulgar, not couthy and fine. He was jealous as hell of the real folk that wrote, Annie S. Swan and that David Lyall: you could read and enjoy ever bit that they wrote, it was fine, clean stuff, not sickening you, like, with dirt about women having bairns and screaming or old men dying in the hills at night or the fear of a sheep as the butcher came. That was the stuff Ake Ogilvie wrote, and who wanted to know about stuff like that? You did a bit of reading to get away from life.

The subject-matter dismissed by the gossips as *dirt* in Ake Ogilvie's poems is the subject-matter of Lewis Grassic Gibbon's *Sunset Song*.

The last sentences of *A Scots Quair* have Chris on a hilltop near the place where she was born as night is falling. *Touns* = farmsteads, *tirred* = undressed, *peeks* = tiny flames.

> Lights had sprung up far in the hills, in little touns for a sunset minute while the folk tirred and went off to their beds, miles away, thin peeks in the summer dark.

> Time she went home herself.
>
> But she sat on as one by one the lights went out and the rain came back, beating the stones about her, and falling all that night while she still sat there, presently feeling no longer the touch of the rain or hearing the sound of the lapwings going by.

She seems to have died of an unspecified disease, but it is a death that seems very like waiting.

From the earliest days of the industrial revolution to the late 1960s most Scots lived in a midland belt containing many large towns and two cities devoted to mining, weaving, pottery and heavy industry: despite which every author discussed in this book since the days of Burns grew up mainly or partly on a farm or in a small country town, with the exception of Robert Louis Stevenson. Why, and what Scottish writers were to make of the last half of the 20th century, must wait for a fuller version of this book.

Notes

Canongate Classics no. 63, *The House with the Green Shutters* by George Douglas Brown, introduced by Cairns Craig, 1996.

Canongate Classics no. 48, *Gillespie* by John MacDougall Hay, introduced by Bob Tait and Isobel Murray, 1993.

The Complete Poems of Hugh MacDiarmid, edited by Michael Grieve and W.R. Aitken, 2 vols, Carcanet, Manchester 1993.

Canongate Classics no. 59, *A Scots Quair* (*Sunset Song, Cloud Howe, Grey Granite*) by Lewis Grassic Gibbon, edited and introduced by Tom Crawford, 1995.

Afterword

THIS BOOK MAY suffer from Scots Wha Haeism, a habit of hinting that the best things come from MY nation. This is a bad habit when it leads to demeaning other nations, but good when it gives folk confidence they need to work well with local material. In 19th-century Russia writers were divided between those who thought their land would only improve by learning from France, Germany and Britain, and those who thought Russia had resources that could make her an example to everyone else. Dostoevsky belonged to the latter school, but justified it with arguments all can accept. Yes (he said – I quote from memory) many Russians do believe that God has chosen them, as he chose the Jews, to make a new and better world, but every nation in the world can only make great and good things by believing God has especially chosen them to do so. That kind of nationalism becomes dangerous, of course, when it turns into imperialism and declares that Britain, Germany, Russia, Israel et cetera can improve the world by seizing control of India, France, Poland, bits of Palestine et cetera, or when it decides that religious or racial minorities inside a nation should be classed as outsiders. But no Scottish empire threatens its neighbours, nor do Catholic, Jewish, Hindu and Moslem Scots find life more dangerous here than in most other nations. They too, if they enjoy the works I describe, will regard them as their property, if they have not already done so.

But I admire above everyone else Jesus Christ and Tom Paine who were derided and rejected for refusing to identify with any national group smaller than humanity. Having concentrated on Scottish writing for the duration of this book I will now spend a long time enjoying books from other lands.

Thank goodness so many exist.

A Short Bibliography

LITERARY HISTORY

The History of Scottish Literature, 4 vols, general editor Cairns Craig (Aberdeen: Aberdeen University Press):

Vol. 1, *Medieval and Renaissance*, ed. R.D. Jack, 1988

Vol. 2, *1660–1800*, ed. Andrew Hook, 1987

Vol. 3, *Nineteenth Century*, ed. Douglas Gifford, 1988

Vol. 4, *Twentieth Century*, ed. Cairns Craig, 1987

Bill Findlay, *A History of Scottish Theatre* (Edinburgh: Polygon, 1998).

Douglas Gifford and Dorothy McMillan, *A History of Scottish Women's Writing* (Edinburgh: Edinburgh University Press, 1997).

Maurice Lindsay, *History of Scottish Literature* (London: Robert Hale, 1977).

Derick S. Thomson, *An Introduction to Gaelic Poetry* (Edinburgh: Edinburgh University Press, 1989).

Marshall Walker, *Scottish Literature Since 1707* (London: Longman, 1996).
Roderick Watson, *The Literature of Scotland* (Basingstoke: Macmillan, 1984).

GUIDES AND COMPANIONS

David Daiches, ed., *A New Companion to Scottish Culture* (Edinburgh: Polygon, 1993).
Trevor Royle, *The Mainstream Companion to Scottish Literature* (Edinburgh: Mainstream, 1993).
Derick S. Thomson, *The Companion to Gaelic Scotland* (Glasgow: Gairm, 1994).

ANTHOLOGIES

Thomas Owen Clancy, *The Triumph Tree* (Edinburgh: Canongate Classics, 1998).
The New Penguin Book of Scottish Verse, ed. Robert Crawford (London: Penguin, 2001).
R.D.S. Jack and P.A.T. Rozendaal, *The Mercat Anthology of Early Scottish Literature, 1375–1707* (Edinburgh: Mercat Press, 1997).
Emily Lyle, ed., *Scottish Ballads* (Edinburgh: Canongate Classics, 1994).
Dream State. The New Scottish Poets, ed. Daniel O'Rourke (Edinburgh: Polygon, 1994).

J.A. Tasioulas, ed., *The Makars: The Poems of Henryson, Dunbar and Douglas* (Edinburgh: Canongate Classics, 1999).

Derick S. Thomson, *Gaelic Poetry in the Eighteenth Century: A Bilingual Anthology* (Aberdeen: Association for Scottish Literary Studies, 1993).

Roderick Watson, *The Poetry of Scotland: Gaelic, Scots and English 1380–1980* (Edinburgh: Edinburgh University Press, 1995).

HISTORY

Thomas M. Devine, *The Scottish Nation 1700–2000* (London: Allan Lane, 1999).

Michael Lynch, *Scotland. A New History* (London: Century, 1991).

REFERENCE

John and Julia Keay, eds, *Collins Encyclopaedia of Scotland* (London: Harper Collins, 1994).

Not all of these are in print, but all are worth reading.

Canongate Classics

Books listed in alphabetical order by author:

The Bruce John Barbour, AAM Duncan (ed.)
ISBN 0 86241 681 7 £9.99
The Land of the Leal James Barke
ISBN 0 86241 142 4 £7.99
Farewell Miss Julie Logan: A JM Barrie Omnibus
(The Little White Bird, The Twelve-Pound Look, Farewell Miss Julie Logan)
JM Barrie
ISBN 0 84195 003 3 £7.99
The Scottish Enlightenment: An Anthology
A Broadie (ed.)
ISBN 0 86241 738 4 £10.99
The House with the Green Shutters
George Douglas Brown
ISBN 0 86241 549 7 £5.99
Magnus George Mackay Brown
ISBN 0 86241 814 3 £5.99
The Leithen Stories (The Power-House, John Macnab, The Dancing Floor, Sick Heart River)
John Buchan
ISBN 0 86241 995 6 £8.99

The Watcher by the Threshold: Shorter Scottish Fiction
John Buchan
ISBN 0 86241 682 5 £7.99
Witchwood John Buchan
ISBN 0 86241 202 1 £6.99
The Life of Robert Burns Catherine Carswell
ISBN 0 86241 292 7 £6.99
Lying Awake Catherine Carswell
ISBN 0 86241 683 3 £5.99
Open the Door! Catherine Carswell
ISBN 0 86241 644 2 £5.99
The Triumph Tree: Scotland's Earliest Poetry 550–1350
Thomas Owen Clancy (ed.)
ISBN 0 86241 787 2 £9.99
Twentieth-Century Scottish Drama: An Anthology
Craig/Stevenson (eds)
ISBN 0 86241 979 4 £12.99
Two Worlds David Daiches
ISBN 0 86241 704 X £5.99
The Complete Brigadier Gerard Arthur Conan Doyle
ISBN 0 86241 534 9 £6.99
A Glasgow Trilogy George Friel
ISBN 086241 885 2 £9.99
Dance of the Apprentices Edward Gaitens
ISBN 0 86241 297 8 £7.99

Ringan Gilhaize John Galt
ISBN 0 86241 552 7 £6.99
The Member and the Radical John Galt
ISBN 0 86241 642 6 £5.99
Memoirs of a Highland Lady vols I & II
Elizabeth Grant of Rothiemurchus
ISBN 0 86241 396 6 £8.99
The Highland Lady in Ireland
Elizabeth Grant of Rothiemurchus
ISBN 0 86241 361 3 £8.99
A Scots Quair (Sunset Song, Cloud Howe, Grey Granite) Lewis Grassic Gibbon
ISBN 0 86241 532 2 £6.99
Smeddum: A Lewis Grassic Gibbon Anthology
Valentina Bold (ed.)
ISBN 0 86241 965 4 £11.99
Sunset Song Lewis Grassic Gibbon
ISBN 0 86241 179 3 £4.99
Unlikely Stories, Mostly Alasdair Gray
ISBN 0 86241 737 6 £6.99
Highland River Neil M. Gunn
ISBN 0 86241 358 3 £5.99
The Key of the Chest Neil M. Gunn
ISBN 0 86241 770 8 £6.99
The Serpent Neil M. Gunn
ISBN 0 86241 728 7 £6.99

Sun Circle Neil M. Gunn
ISBN 0 86241 587 X £6.99
The Well at the World's End Neil M. Gunn
ISBN 0 86241 645 0 £5.99
Gillespie J. MacDougall Hay
ISBN 0 86241 427 X £6.99
The Private Memoirs and Confessions of a Justified Sinner
James Hogg
ISBN 0 86241 340 0 £5.99
The Three Perils of Man James Hogg
ISBN 0 86241 646 9 £8.99
Flemington & Tales from Angus Violet Jacob
ISBN 0 86241 784 8 £8.99
Fergus Lamont Robin Jenkins
ISBN 0 86241 310 9 £6.99
Just Duffy Robin Jenkins
ISBN 0 86241 551 9 £5.99
The Changeling Robin Jenkins
ISBN 0 86241 228 5 £5.99
Journey to the Hebrides (A Journey to the Western Isles of Scotland, The Journal of a Tour to the Hebrides)
Samuel Johnson & James Boswell
ISBN 0 86241 588 8 £6.99
Household Ghosts: A James Kennaway Omnibus
(Tunes of Glory, Household Ghosts, Silence)

James Kennaway
ISBN 1 84195 125 0 £7.99

Wisdom, Madness and Folly RD Laing
ISBN 0 86241 831 3 £5.99

The Haunted Woman David Lindsay
ISBN 0 86241 162 9 £6.99

A Voyage to Arcturus David Lindsay
ISBN 0 86241 377 X £6.99

Ane Satyre of the Thrie Estaitis
Sir David Lindsay
ISBN 0 86241 191 2 £4.99

The Dark of Summer Eric Linklater
ISBN 0 86241 894 1 £5.99

Magnus Merriman Eric Linklater
ISBN 0 86241 313 3 £6.99

Private Angelo Eric Linklater
ISBN 0 86241 376 1 £5.99

Scottish Ballads Emily Lyle (ed.)
ISBN 0 86241 477 6 £5.99

Nua-Bhardachd Ghaidhlig/
Modern Scottish Gaelic Poems
Donald MacAulay (ed.)
ISBN 0 86241 494 6 £4.99

The Early Life of James McBey James McBey
ISBN 0 86241 445 8 £5.99

Three Scottish Poets MacCaig, Morgan, Lochhead
ISBN 0 86241 400 8 £6.99

And the Cock Crew Fionn MacColla
ISBN 0 86241 536 5 £4.99
The Devil and the Giro: Two Centuries of Scottish Stories
Carl MacDougall (ed.)
ISBN 0 86241 359 1 £9.99
St Kilda: Island on the Edge of the World
Charles Maclean
ISBN 0 86241 388 5 £6.99
Linmill Stories Robert McLellan
ISBN 0 86241 282 X £6.99
Homeward Journey John MacNair Reid
ISBN 0 86241 178 5 £3.95
The Silver Bough F. Marian McNeill
ISBN 0 86241 231 5 £6.99
Wild Harbour Ian Macpherson
ISBN 0 86241 234 X £6.99
A Childhood in Scotland Christian Miller
ISBN 0 86241 230 7 £4.99
The Blood of the Martyrs Naomi Mitchison
ISBN 0 86241 192 0 £8.99
The Corn King and the Spring Queen
Naomi Mitchison
ISBN 0 86241 287 0 £9.99
The Gowk Storm Nancy Brysson Morrison
ISBN 0 86241 222 6 £4.99

An Autobiography Edwin Muir
ISBN 0 86241 423 7 £6.99

The Wilderness Journeys (The Story of My Boyhood and Youth, A Thousand Mile Walk to the Gulf, My First Summer in the Sierra, Travels in Alaska, Stickeen) John Muir
ISBN 0 86241 586 1 £9.99

Imagined Selves (Imagined Corners, Mrs Ritchie, Mrs Grundy in Scotland, Women: An Inquiry, Women in Scotland) Willa Muir
ISBN 0 86241 605 1 £8.99

A Beleaguered City: Tales of the Seen and Unseen Margaret Oliphant
ISBN 1 84195 060 2 £7.99

A Twelvemonth and a Day Christopher Rush
ISBN 0 86241 439 3 £6.99

The End of an Old Song J.D. Scott
ISBN 0 86241 311 7 £4.95

The Journal of Sir Walter Scott WEK Anderson (ed.)
ISBN 0 86241 828 3 £12.99

The Grampian Quartet (The Quarry Wood, The Weatherhouse, A Pass in the Grampians, The Living Mountain) Nan Shepherd
ISBN 0 86241 589 6 £9.99

Consider the Lilies Iain Crichton Smith
ISBN 0 86241 415 6 £4.99

Listen to the Voice: Selected Stories
Iain Crichton Smith
ISBN 0 86241 434 2 £7.99

Diaries of a Dying Man William Soutar
ISBN 0 86241 347 8 £6.99

Markheim, Jekyll and the Merry Men: Shorter Scottish Fiction
Robert Louis Stevenson
ISBN 0 86241 555 1 £6.99

Tales of Adventure (Black Arrow, Treasure Island, 'The Sire de Malétroit's Door' and other stories)
Robert Louis Stevenson
ISBN 0 86241 687 6 £7.99

Tales of the South Seas (Island Landfalls, The Ebb-tide, The Wrecker) Robert Louis Stevenson
ISBN 0 86241 643 4 £7.99

The Scottish Novels (Kidnapped, Catriona, The Master of Ballantrae, Weir of Hermiston) Robert Louis Stevenson
ISBN 0 86241 533 0 £6.99

The Makars: The Poems of Henryson, Dunbar and Douglas
JA Tasioulas (ed.)
ISBN 0 86241 820 8 £9.99

Divided Loyalties Janet Teissier du Cros
ISBN 0 86241 375 3 £8.99

The Bad Sister: An Emma Tennant Omnibus (The Bad Sister, Two Women of London, Wild Nights) Emma Tennant
ISBN 1 84195 053 X £7.99

The People of the Sea David Thomson
ISBN 1 84195 107 2 £6.99

The City of Dreadful Night James Thomson
ISBN 0 86241 449 0 £5.99

Black Lamb and Grey Falcon Rebecca West
ISBN 0 86241 428 8 £12.99

The King and the Lamp: Scottish Traveller Tales Duncan and Linda Williamson
ISBN 1 84195 063 7 £7.99